ranjini's kitchen

MY FAVOURITE R

RANJINI WOODHOUSE

SOULJOURNEY PUBLISHING

First Edition
Published by Souljourney Publishing
September 2014

ISBN: 978-0-9570251-4-1

First Edition published by Souljouney Publishing

Illustration Copyright © 2014 James Woodhouse

Cover Design, Interior Design and Layout
James Woodhouse & Michael Hooper

To my dedicated and loyal taste testers:

my husband John
and my children James and Zoë

contents

introduction

Following on from my first book, *'My Favourite Curries'*, the idea for the second cookbook was inspired by friends asking for non-curry recipes that they have tried in my house. This second cookbook is of my favourite recipes of dishes that I have cooked during my stay in Singapore, Hong Kong and the UK since my marriage. I have also included some of my family's favourite recipes.

There are a few unique things about this book:

There are western and eastern recipes and most of them are quick and easy dishes each designed to serve 3 - 4 people.

I hope you enjoy cooking and eating the dishes in this book.

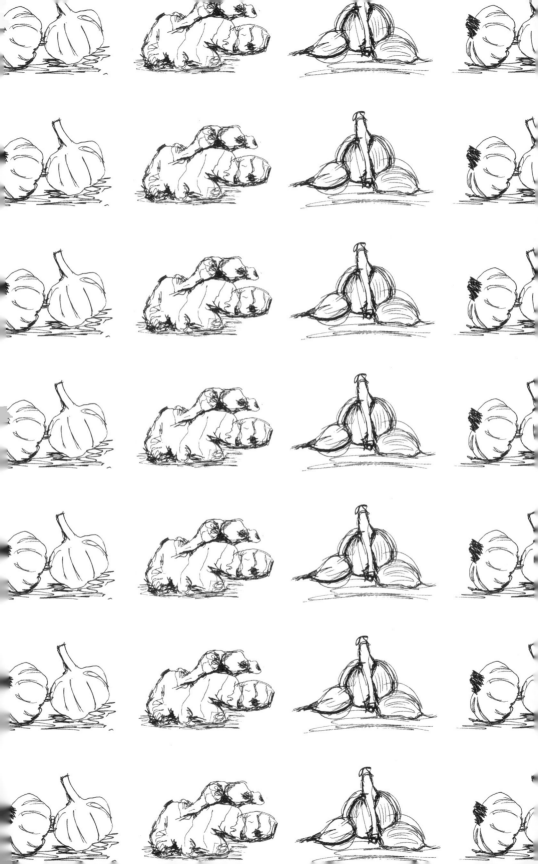

for every food lovers kitchen

general / non herbs

garlic
It has a very pungent and very piercing flavour. It can be used in salad dressings, butter, as a base for sauces, casseroles and soups. Whole garlic bulbs can be roasted with meat to add flavour.

lemon
Lemon is one of the most versatile fruits and contains a high level of vitamin C. The flesh is a little too sour to eat on its own. The tartness of the juice is wonderful to combine with all sweet and savoury dishes.

ginger
It has a mild pungent taste. Raw ginger is used in curries, stir fry dishes or to make ginger tea. Dried ginger is used in cakes, biscuits and desserts.

lime
A small green citrus fruit used mainly in Asian cooking. It has a stronger more bitter taste than lemon. It can also be used with all sweet and savoury dishes.

herbs

basil
A versatile aromatic herb used widely in Southern Europe and many parts of Asia. There are many varieties of basil. Holy basil (tulsi) is an essential part of Indian and Thai cooking. Compliments tomato based dishes.

coriander
The coriander seeds give dishes a warm, aromatic and slightly citrus flavour. Fresh coriander leaves or cilantro is used in Asian and Mediterranean cooking. It has a totally different flavour to dried coriander seeds. The leaves are usually added as a garnish.

cayenne pepper
A pungent powder made from various tropical chillies. Generally used in soups and sauces.

herbes de Provence
Herbes de Provence is a fragrant mixture of dried herbs typical of Southern French cooking. Exact recipes vary, but thyme, savory, rosemary and fennel or tarragon are typical ingredients. Marjoram, basil or lavender flowers may be included in the mixture.

chives
It is a member of the onion family. It has a mild, grassy flavour similar to baby spring onions or young leeks. It compliments eggs, fish, soups and salads. There is also an Asian variety of chives called Chinese chives, garlic chives or kuchai.

for every food lovers kitchen

mint
There are many different species of mint such as spearmint, pineapple mint, lemon mint, chocolate mint, peppermint. The one used most widely in western cooking is spearmint. Peppermint is used to flavour ice cream, sweets and confectionary.

mixed herbs
Mixed herbs may consist of a combination of parsley, rosemary, basil, marjoram, thyme and oregano. Used in sauces, stews and soups.

mustard
Black mustard seeds have a very sharp pungent taste. It is used in pickles, chutneys and certain meat, fish and vegetable dishes.

oregano
A pungent green herb closely related to marjoram. It is used to compliment any tomato based dishes.

paprika
Paprika is the ground bright red powder from sweet and hot dried peppers. It is much milder than cayenne pepper with a slight sweetness. Smoked or un-smoked paprika brings a distinct flavour to the dishes it is added to.

parsley
This is a multi-purpose herb no kitchen should be without. It can be used as a garnish, flavouring and as a vegetable. The flat leaf parsley has a stronger flavour than the curly parsley.

rosemary
It has an intense fragrant aroma. It is traditionally used with lamb, chicken and game. It is used in French, Spanish, Italian and Mediterranean cooking.

sage
Traditionally sage is used as a stuffing to flavour fatty meats such as pork, goose and sausages. It can also be added to pasta sauces and used for poultry stuffing. It is never used raw.

tarragon
Used in French cooking has a distinctive aniseed flavour.

thyme
It has a heady aromatic flavour and comes in different varieties with flavours of mint, lemon, and stronger varieties that taste more like oregano. It is used in stuffing and marinades.

soups

....

beetroot and coconut
butternut squash
carrot and coriander
chicken and sweet corn
chicken and vegetable
cream of mushroom
curried parsnip
laksa
leek and potato
new england clam chowder
pumpkin and black pepper
ranjini's mullagutanny
tom yam
won ton

beetroot and coconut soup

2 small onions, sliced
1 tbsp olive oil
1 carrot, chopped
½ tsp minced ginger
1 green chilli, finely chopped
1 lemongrass, chopped
5-6 lime leaves
1 beetroot, finely chopped
250 ml vegetable stock
Salt and pepper to taste
200 ml coconut milk
1 tbsp cream
1 tbsp rice or white vinegar

In a pot heat the olive oil and add the onions and minced ginger.
Cook onions until slightly golden in colour.
Add the green chilli, lemon grass, lime leaves and mix well.
Add the beetroot.
Add the vinegar and the stock.
Add the coconut milk and mix.
Add pepper and salt to taste.
Let it simmer for about 10 minutes.
Blend the soup in a blender.
Top with a swirl of cream before serving.

butternut squash soup

1 large onion, sliced
200 g chickpea flour
1 tsp baking powder
2 tbsp rice flour
½ tsp chilli powder
½ tsp turmeric powder
½ tsp cumin powder
½ tsp coriander powder
100 ml water
750 ml vegetable oil
Salt to taste

Pre-heat the oven to 180 degrees C.
Cut the squash lengthways into quarters, remove seeds.
Arrange on a baking tray.
Drizzle with olive oil.
Sprinkle the chilli flakes and cumin seeds on the butternut squash.
Add a little salt and pepper.
Roast in the oven for 40 to 50 minutes.
Leave the squash to cool before peeling the skin.
Heat the butter in a pan.
Add the garlic and onions and cook until soft.
Pour in the stock and simmer gently.
Add the chunks of butternut squash.
Gently simmer for five minutes.
Blend in a blender until it is smooth.
Return to pan.
Add salt and pepper to taste.
If it is too thick, add a couple of tablespoons of milk.
Serve soup with swirls of crème fraîche and sprinkling of ground nutmeg.

carrot and coriander soup

½ tbsp vegetable oil
½ an onion, sliced
225g carrots, sliced
½ tsp ground coriander
600 ml vegetable stock
Fresh coriander leaves, chopped
Salt to taste
Freshly ground black pepper

Heat the oil in a large pan.
Add the onions and the carrots.
Cook for 3 to 4 minutes until soft.
Stir in the ground coriander and season well.
Cook for 1 minute.
Add the vegetable stock and bring to the boil.
Lower heat and let it simmer for a few minutes.
Blend until smooth with a hand blender or in a blender.
Reheat in a clean pan.
Stir in the fresh coriander and serve.

chicken and sweetcorn soup

200g minced chicken
1 egg white
2 tbsp water
440g can creamed sweet corn
3 cups chicken stock
1 tsp sesame oil
1 tsp soy sauce
1 ½ tbsp corn starch
¼ cup water – extra

Combine the chicken, egg white and 2 tablespoons of water in a bowl.
Mix well and let it stand for 10 minutes.
Combine the sweet corn, the stock, soy sauce and oil in a pan.
Cook on a gentle heat.
Stir while cooking, boil uncovered for 3 minutes.
Dissolve the corn starch in quarter cup of water.
Add to the soup and stir until the soup boils and thickens.
Add the chicken mixture.
Cook for 2 minutes stir constantly.

Not suitable for freezing or microwaving.

chicken and vegetable soup

4 chicken thigh and leg cut into pieces
1 vegetable stock cube
Dash of aromat
1 carrot, cubed
1 onion, cubed
5-6 beans, cut
2 potatoes, cubed
Cauliflower florets
Broccoli florets
Salt and pepper to taste

In frying pan heat a little oil and brown the chicken pieces.
In a large pan, add the diced vegetables, sufficient water and a vegetable stock cube.
Add the chicken, salt, pepper and aromat and cook.
Serve hot.

cream of mushroom soup

60g butter
1 small onion, diced
4 stalks celery, diced
1 leek, chopped
200g mushrooms, chopped
3 tbsp flour
340 ml milk
460 ml vegetable stock
Freshly ground pepper
Salt to taste

Melt the butter in a pan over a low heat.
Add the diced onion, celery, leek and mushrooms.
Cook for about 5 minutes without allowing them to colour.
When the vegetables are soft and onions translucent, add the flour and mix well.
Pour in the milk and the vegetable stock and stir.
Add salt and pepper to taste.
Let the soup cook for 20 to 25 minutes.
Leave the soup to cool slightly.
Pour it into a blender and blend until smooth.
Reheat soup before serving.

curried parsnip soup

½ an onion
150g parsnips
½ a carrot
½ a potato
25g butter
1 tbsp plain flour
1 tbsp curry powder
600ml vegetable stock
2 tbsp crème fraîche
Handful parsley, chopped

Peel and roughly chop all the vegetables, keep the onion separate.
Melt the butter in a large saucepan.
Add the onions, and cook until soft.
Add the other vegetables, followed by the flour and curry powder.
Stir well and cook for a further 2 minutes.
Gradually add the stock stirring until well blended.
Increase the heat and bring to the boil and reduce the heat to a low simmer.
Cover and leave to cook 40 minutes, or until the vegetables are tender.
Turn the heat off, uncover, and allow the soup to cool slightly.
Pour the soup into a blender and blitz until completely smooth.
Reheat before serving.
Garnish each bowl with a swirl of crème fraîche and chopped parsley.

laksa
....

spice paste

4 shallots, peeled and chopped
2 cloves garlic, peeled and chopped
25g fresh ginger, peeled and chopped
1 stalk lemongrass, chopped
3 candlenuts
1tsp shrimp paste
2 dried red chillies, soaked and deseeded
1 tsp palm sugar
1 tbsp dried shrimps, soaked until soft
½ tbsp vegetable oil
3 shallots, peeled and finely sliced

Using a pestle and mortar or a blender grind all the ingredients, except the oil and the 3 sliced shallots into a paste.
Add the oil to the paste, mix well.
Put aside.

soup base

300 ml coconut milk
200 ml chicken stock
1 cups water
50g fresh squid, sliced
2 hard boiled eggs, shelled and quartered
1½ tbsp oil
125g yellow noodles – boiled
125g vermicelli – boiled
Handful of bean sprouts
Chilli oil
50g peeled prawns
A small bunch coriander or mint, roughly chopped
Salt to taste

other

Oil for deep frying

Heat the oil in a wok and deep fry shallots until crisp and golden.
Drain on paper towels and set aside.
To a pan add half a tablespoon of oil and stir in spice paste.
Cook over low heat for 3 to 4 minutes, until fragrant.
Add coconut milk and chicken stock.
Bring to the boil, stirring all the time.
Add the prawns and squid.
Simmer gently until cooked.
Add salt and pepper to taste.
To serve, divide noodles among individual bowls.
Add bean sprouts; pour over the soup and seafood.
Garnish with crispy fried shallots, coriander or mint leaves, and a drizzle of chilli oil.

leek and potato soup

1 large white onion
2 stalks celery
4 medium leeks
1 tbsp butter
1 tbsp olive oil
1500 ml vegetable stock
3 potatoes
Small bunch of fresh thyme
150 ml crème fraîche
Sea salt and ground black pepper to taste
1 garlic clove, chopped

Peel and roughly chop the onion.
Trim and roughly chop the celery.
Trim the leeks cut into chunks and rinse well.
In a deep pan, melt a little butter.
Add the chopped garlic and vegetables except the potatoes, a little olive oil and a splash of water.
Cover with a lid and cook for 8 to10 minutes, or until the vegetables have softened.
In another pan simmer the vegetable stock.
Peel the potatoes then roughly chop into small pieces.
Add to the pan of simmering stock and cook for 5 minutes with the thyme stalks.
When the potatoes are cooked, take the thyme stalks out.
Pour the stock mixture into the pan of softened vegetables.
Bring to the boil.
Take off fire.
Pour it into a blender and blend until smooth.
Add salt and pepper to taste.
Serve in bowls with a swirl of crème fraîche and thyme leaves on top.

New England clam chowder

¼ cup diced bacon
¼ cup minced onion
250g mashed potato
1 cup milk
2 cans minced clams
1 tbsp lemon juice
Freshly ground pepper

Cook bacon and onion until bacon is crisp and onion is tender.
Add the milk and mashed potato and stir.
Let it simmer for a few minutes.
Stir occasionally.
Add the clams with the liquid, lemon juice and pepper.
Heat through well.

pumpkin and black pepper soup

20 ml olive oil
5 tbsp chopped onions
2 tbsp chopped celery
2 tsp chopped garlic
2 bay leaves
200g pumpkin, cleaned and diced
5 peppercorns
Salt to taste
20 ml white wine
4 cups vegetable stock
20 ml fresh cream
¼ tsp freshly ground black pepper

Heat the oil in a pan.
Add the onion, celery, garlic and bay leaf.
Sauté until the onion is light brown in colour.
Add the diced pumpkin and peppercorns and cook until the vegetables are soft.
Add salt and pepper to taste.
Add the white wine and vegetable stock and cook for 25 minutes, or until the pumpkin is soft and pulpy.
Remove from heat and puree it.
Return to heat.
Add the fresh cream and freshly ground black pepper, simmer for a further 5 minutes.
Serve hot, garnished with olive oil and a swirl of cream.

Ranjini's mulagutanny soup

1 large chicken
4 tomatoes, chopped
1 onion, chopped
3 cups of water
2 cloves garlic, chopped
1 cm ginger, chopped
1 cm piece of cinnamon
6-8 cloves
1 tsp cumin
Curry leaves
½ tsp turmeric powder
½ tsp fenugreek
½ cup coconut milk
1 tbsp lemon juice
20 peppercorns

Cut chicken into pieces.
Smash the chicken pieces with a meat tenderiser.
In a pan add all the ingredients except the coconut milk and lemon juice.
Bring to boil.
Turn down the heat and let the soup simmer for 30 to 40 minutes.
Add the coconut milk.
Cook for 3 to 4 minutes.
Take off fire and add a little lemon juice before serving.

Mulagu means pepper and thanny means water, in Tamil a language spoken
in Sri Lanka.

tom yam soup

4-6 cups chicken stock
1 stalk lemongrass, minced
3 kaffir lime leaves
3-4 cloves garlic, minced
1-2 red chillies, finely sliced
3 tbsp fish sauce
Cherry tomatoes, halved
4-5 fresh shitake mushroom, sliced
12 medium raw shrimps, shelled
1 tbsp lime juice
1/3 cup fresh coriander leaves
300 ml chicken stock
200 ml coconut milk or 200 ml evaporated milk

Pour chicken stock into a deep cooking pot and bring to a boil.
Add the lemongrass and boil for 1 to 2 minutes.
Add garlic, chilli, lime leaves, and mushrooms.
Reduce heat to medium and simmer for 1 to 2 minutes.
Add the shrimps plus the vegetables.
Simmer for 3 to 4 minutes, or until shrimps are pink and plump.
Reduce heat to medium-low and add the coconut milk.
Add the fish sauce and lime juice.
Stir well to combine.
Gently simmer until hot.
Serve in bowls sprinkled with chopped coriander.
Add a little Thai chilli sauce if desired.

won ton soup

18 - 24 won ton wrappers

filling

250g boneless lean pork, finely chopped
1 tbsp soy sauce
1 tbsp oyster sauce
A few drops of sesame oil
1 tsp rice wine
½ tsp sugar
1 spring onion, finely minced
1 tsp corn starch
¼ tsp white pepper

other

Water for boiling won tons
4 ½-5 cups chicken stock
Spring onions, thinly sliced
A few drops sesame oil

Mix all the filling ingredients in a bowl.
Take one won ton skin and place it on a flat surface.
Cover the rest of the won ton skins with a damp towel to prevent them from drying out.
Place a heaped teaspoon of the filling in the centre of the won ton skin.
Moisten all the edges with water.
Twist won ton skin to seal.
It should resemble a draw string bag.
Bring a large pot of water to a boil.
Gently lower the won tons few at a time.
When they rise to the top of the water, the filling is cooked through, about 5 to 8 minutes.
Remove the won tons from the pot with a slotted spoon.

soup

Bring the chicken stock to a boil.
Add the won tons and bring the soup back to a boil.
Add the spring onions.
Remove from fire.
Add sesame oil.
Serve in bowls with six won tons per bowl.

The name won ton means swallowing a cloud. The won tons floating in this

popular soup are thought to resemble clouds.

salads

....

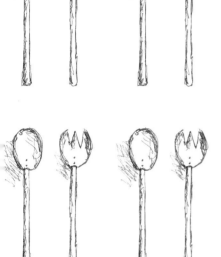

asian coleslaw
carrot and coriander
chicken and apple
chicken caesar
chicken waldorf
chilli prawn
chinese chicken
crunchy thai salad with cashew nuts
gado-gado
mung bean noodle
nutty coleslaw
papaya
prawns and mango
rice salad
rojak

asian coleslaw

1 cup grated carrots
1 cup grated green cabbage
1 cup grated red cabbage
1 cup precooked edamame beans
1½ cups water
Spicy soy sesame dressing
Almonds, thinly sliced
Toasted sesame seeds
Chilli flakes

Bring the water to boil.
Lightly blanch the precooked
edamame beans for one minute.
Remove and drain.
Chill in the refrigerator.

spicy soy sesame dressing

¼ cup light soy sauce
½ cup brown sugar
¼ cup sesame oil
2 tbsp almond butter
2 tbsp apple cider vinegar
1 tbsp rice vinegar
2 tsp toasted sesame seeds
1-2 tbsp chilli flakes
Salt and sugar to taste

Mix all the dressing ingredients and
season to taste.

almond butter

300g almonds with skin
Good drizzle of honey

Preheat oven to 170 degrees C.
Spread almonds on a baking tray and roast for 10 minutes.
Remove and cool.
In a food processes whizz the almonds until broken into tiny pieces.
Add a little honey and mix well.

In a salad bowl mix all the vegetables and the edamame beans.
Spoon a generous amount of the dressing over it and stir well.
Chill in the refrigerator until ready to serve.
Just before serving, add extra dressing, toasted sesame seeds, almond butter and
chilli flakes.

Almond butter stores well in refrigerator for 3 weeks.

carrot and coriander salad

4 carrots, peeled and grated
½ orange, juiced
1 lemon, juiced
1 tsp sesame oil
2 tbsp chopped coriander
Salt and pepper to taste

Whisk the orange and lemon juices with the sesame oil.
Add salt and pepper to taste.
Pour over the carrots and let it stand for 10 minutes.
Mix well and stir in the coriander leaves just before serving.

chicken and apple salad

salad

2 cups chicken pieces, cooked
2 cups chopped lettuce leaves
2 cups apple, peeled and cubed
¼ cup strawberries, halved
½ cup cheddar cheese, cubed
2 tbsp raisins

dressing

¼ cup vegetable oil
¼ cup cider vinegar
2 tbsp sugar
1/8 tbsp cinnamon powder

Mix together the dressing ingredients.
Mix all the salad ingredients, except the raisins.
Pour the dressing over the salad.
Toss well.
Garnish with raisins and serve immediately.

chicken caesar salad

....

caesar salad dressing

25g can anchovies
1½ tbsp fresh lemon juice
½ tbsp Worcestershire sauce
½ tsp chopped parsley
½ tsp Dijon mustard
¼ tsp freshly ground black pepper
1 clove garlic, crushed
¼ cup olive oil
2 tbsp freshly grated Parmesan cheese

Mash the anchovies in a bowl, stir in the lemon juice, Worcestershire sauce, chopped parsley, Dijon mustard, garlic and pepper.
Whisk in the olive oil slowly.
Stir in 2 tablespoons freshly grated Parmesan cheese.

caesar salad

250g skinless chicken breasts
½ cup Caesar salad dressing
Freshly grated Parmesan cheese
Freshly ground pepper
Garlic flavoured croutons
2-3 rashers of crispy fried bacon (optional)
1 small romaine lettuce torn into bite size pieces

Grill the chicken on medium heat for 15-20 minutes, turning once.
Cut the chicken pieces diagonally into 1 cm slices.
Pour the dressing into a bowl.
Add the romaine lettuce and toss to coat.
Sprinkle the croutons, cheese and the freshly ground pepper.
Toss the salad.
Place the chicken pieces on top of the salad and serve.

chicken Waldorf salad

salad

5 black peppercorns
1 bay leaf
1 garlic, halved
4 chicken breasts
2 spring onions
1 stalk celery
2 red apples
¼ cup toasted walnuts

dressing

½ cup plain yogurt
1/3 cup light mayonnaise
2 tbsp fresh parsley chopped
2 tsp lemon juice
2 tsp Dijon mustard
¼ tsp pepper

In small bowl, whisk together, mayonnaise, yogurt, parsley, lemon juice, mustard and pepper. (Dressing can be covered and refrigerated for up to 8 hours.)

To a large shallow saucepan add the peppercorns, bay leaf, garlic and a little water.
Heat until it is simmering.
Add the chicken to the pan in a single layer, meaty side down.
Cook for 15-20 minutes or until no longer pink inside.
Transfer the chicken to a plate and let it cool.
Refrigerate for about 1 hour.
(Chicken can be covered and stored for up to 4 hours.)
Remove the skin from chicken.
Cut lengthwise into strips and then into cubes.
Thinly slice the spring onions and celery.
Wash and cut apples into cubes.
In large bowl, combine chicken, spring onions, celery, apples and walnuts.
Add dressing and stir gently to coat well.

Waldorf salad was created in 1896 by the maître d'hôtel Oscar Tschirky, at

New York's Waldorf-Astoria Hotel. The original version contained only apples, celery

and mayonnaise.

chilli prawn salad

2 tbsp vegetable oil
1 tbsp tomato puree
150g onions, chopped
150g green peppers, chopped
1 green chilli, chopped
2 tbsp chopped fresh coriander
2 tbsp mango chutney
3 tbsp mustard oil
1 tsp sugar
300g large raw prawns, cleaned, peeled and de-veined

Heat the vegetable oil in a large frying pan.
Add the prawns and stir fry for 3 to 4 minutes.
Stir in the tomato puree.
Remove from heat and cool in a bowl for 30 to 40 minutes.
Mix the remaining ingredients.
Season to taste and serve cold with chopped coriander.

Chinese chicken salad

salad

3 boneless chicken breasts cooked and diced
1 head lettuce torn into small pieces
4 spring onions, sliced
4 stalks celery, sliced thin
½ cup walnuts, chopped
2 tbsp sesame seeds, toasted
200g cooked noodles

In a large salad bowl, combine the chicken, lettuce, spring onion, celery, walnuts, sesame seeds and cooked noodles.
Mix all together.
Set aside.

dressing

4 tbsp white sugar
6 tbsp rice vinegar
1 tsp salt
½ cup peanut oil

Put vinegar in a small bowl.
Dissolve sugar and salt in vinegar.
Add the oil.
Whisk it well.
Add dressing to salad and toss to coat.
Serve.

crunchy thai salad with cashew nuts

dressing

1 tbsp lime juice
1 tbsp soy sauce
1 tbsp fish sauce
1 tsp rice vinegar
1-2 tsp sugar to taste
Pinch of pepper
1 fresh red chilli, de-seeded and minced

Mix all the dressing in a bowl.
Set aside.

salad

1 cucumber
1 carrot
1 cup cashew nuts
½ red pepper, sliced
2 spring onions
Fresh coriander
Fresh basil

Cut the cucumber in half and slice thinly.
Add the grated carrot, cashew nuts, red pepper, and spring onions.
Pour the dressing over and toss well.
Add the fresh basil and coriander.

Add shrimps or fried tofu for a main meal salad.

gado-gado

Long green beans, cut and blanched
Chinese cabbage, shredded and blanched
4 potatoes boiled and sliced
Handful of bean sprouts
3 boiled eggs, quartered
Fried tofu
Fried shallots
Shrimp crackers
Lettuce, shredded
Tomato cut into quarters
Cassava chips
Lontong (rice cake in a log shape), cut into 1 cm thick (optional)

sauce

10 cloves garlic, stir fried or roasted
300g roasted peanuts or 1 cup of organic crunchy peanut butter
100 ml coconut milk
10 red chillies deseeded and stir fried
1 tsp dried shrimp paste, toasted
60g palm sugar
2-3 tbsp rice flour dissolved in a small amount of water

Blend in a food processor the garlic, peanuts, half of the coconut milk, red chillies,
shrimp paste and palm sugar.
In a pot, combine the processed mixture with the rest of coconut milk, stir and cook on
a low heat.
Stir occasionally.
Cook until it is reduced and the sauce surface looks a bit oily.
Add rice flour mixture.
Keep stirring until bubbling about 5 minutes.
Remove from the heat.
Serve gado-gado sauce while it is still warm.
Warm up the sauce if it is cold.
Leftover sauce can be kept in a jar in the refrigerator.
Use as a dipping sauce.

gado-gado (continued)

sambal
15-20 red bird eyes chillies, steamed
½ tsp sugar
Sea salt to taste

Combine chillies, sugar and salt in a blender or pestle and mortar and grind.

Place lettuce, slices of lontong (optional), boiled potatoes, blanched vegetables, wedges of boiled egg, slices of fried tofu, wedges of tomato and slices of cucumber. Pour the warm sauce over, garnish with fried shallot, crushed shrimp crackers and cassava chips.
Put sambal on the side.

lontong
Cook ½ cup of rice in the normal way.
Wrap it up like a roll in a banana leaf or foil.
Place in a pan of water and boil for 2-3 hours.
Remove and cut into pieces.

Gado gado means a salad of boiled and raw vegetables dressed with a

peanut and coconut sauce.

mung bean noodle salad

2 small bundles of mung bean noodles
250g fresh prawns, peeled and de-veined
½ cup chicken stock
¼ cup roasted peanuts
1/8 cup dried chillies
Lettuce – iceberg or romaine
1 stalk celery, sliced
½ bunch of fresh coriander
2 spring onions, sliced
1 chilli, sliced
¼ onion, sliced

dressing

Juice of 2 large limes
3-4 tbsp of fish sauce
Mix together.

Soak the bundles of noodles in cold water for at least 10 minutes.
Drain and cut them into smaller strips.
Heat a small pan on low heat.
Roast the peanuts, remove and set aside.
Roast the dry chillies, remove and set aside.
In a larger pan bring one cup of chicken stock to boil.
Add the prawns and cook until they turn pink.
Add the mung bean noodles.
Switch off the heat when the noodles turn transparent.
Transfer the cooked noodles and prawns to a mixing bowl.
Slice the red onion, spring onions, coriander leaves, chillies and celery.
Add to the noodles and prawns.
Pour the dressing over the noodles.
Toss the salad to mix well.
Garnish with roasted peanuts and roasted dried chilli.
Serve on a bed of lettuce.

nutty coleslaw

½ small white cabbage, shredded
2 carrots, peeled and grated
4 celery sticks, chopped
1 crisp dessert apple, chopped
50g seedless raisins
50g roasted cashew nuts
Juice of ½ a lemon
3 tbsp Greek style yogurt
Freshly ground black pepper
Salt to taste

Mix the vegetables, fruits and nuts in a large salad bowl.
Stir in the lemon juice and yogurt and toss the salad.
Add freshly ground black pepper and salt to taste.
Cover and chill until required.

papaya salad

1-2 cloves garlic
1 tsp sugar
3-10 fresh red chillies
A little dried prawns
½ cup roasted peanuts
2 limes
150g long beans
A little fish sauce
Grated raw papaya
2 tomatoes

Pound the garlic, chillies, nuts in a deep pestle and mortar.
Add the papaya, dried prawns, and long beans and pound again.
Add the limes juice, fish sauce and sugar.
Lastly add the tomatoes.
Serve.

If raw papaya is not available use white radish or raw mangoes.

prawns and mango salad

1 red chilli, deseeded and chopped
2 tbsp lime juice
1 tbsp cider vinegar
1 tbsp honey
5 tbsp olive oil
450g king prawns, cooked
1 bag of salad leaves
1 pointed red pepper
¼ cucumber, sliced
4 spring onions
2 firm mangoes peeled and cut into pieces
Salt and pepper to taste

Place the chilli, lime juice, honey and oil in a food processor and blend.
Add salt and pepper to taste.
Pour half the dressing over the prawns cover and chill for 20 minutes.
Place the mango, salad leaves, cucumber and spring onions on four plates.
Top with prawns and serve with the extra dressing.

rice salad

250g frozen peas, cooked
3 cups cooked cooled rice
100g diced red pepper
1 cup diced cooked ham
6 spring onions, chopped
4 hard boiled eggs, chopped
¾ cup pimento stuffed olives
½ cup chopped celery
1/3 cup sweet pickle
2 cups grated cheddar cheese
¼ cup mayonnaise
Lettuce leaves
Cherry tomatoes
Salt and pepper to taste

Combine all the ingredients.
Stir well.
Add mayonnaise tossing until well mixed.
Chill in refrigerator.
Serve with lettuce leaves and garnish with cherry tomatoes.

rojak
....

1 small cucumber, sliced
2 tomatoes, quartered
3 boiled potatoes, quartered
3 hard-boiled eggs, quartered
A handful of lettuce, torn to pieces
1 green chilli, chopped
1 unripe mango, cubed
¼ pineapple, cubed
Sesame seeds
Roasted peanuts

sauce

1 tbsp finely chopped hot chilli
1 tbsp tamarind paste
1 tbsp shrimp paste
1 tbsp oyster sauce
3 tbsp brown sugar
1/3 cup water

Place all the ingredients in a small
saucepan and mix well.
Cook over a low heat until the sugar
dissolves and sauce becomes
slightly thick.
Cool.
Arrange the vegetables, prawn
fritters, eggs and potatoes in a bowl.
Pour the sauce over and serve.

prawn fritters

300g plain flour
½ tsp baking powder
1 egg
2 shallots, finely chopped
Salt and pepper to taste
A little water
200 gm prawns, peeled and chopped coarsely
Oil for frying

Put flour and baking powder in a large bowl.
Add prawns, shallots, pepper, salt and egg.
Mix well.
Add water a little at a time while stirring to
make a smooth medium batter.
Heat oil in wok and drop spoonfuls of batter.
Fry until golden brown.
Remove and drain on paper towel.
When cool, slice the fritters.

Rojak is a mixture of fruit and vegetable salad commonly found in Malaysia,

Singapore and Indonesia.

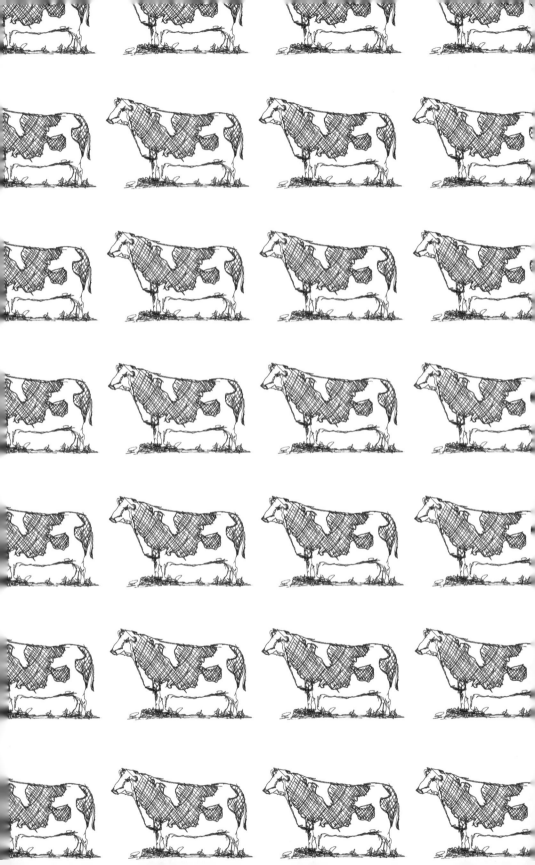

beef

·····················

beef stroganoff
chilli con carne
chunky beef casserole
cottage pie
hamburgers/meatballs
meat loaf
sloppy jo
steak and kidney pie

beef stroganoff

500g beef, cut into thin slices
8 -10 shallots, cut in half
2 cloves garlic, crushed
225g mushrooms, sliced
4 tbsp olive oil
1 tbsp plain flour
1 tbsp tomato puree
Salt and pepper to taste
2 tsp wholegrain or Dijon mustard
200 ml beef stock or water
150 ml sour cream or crème fraîche
1 tbsp chopped flat leaf parsley

Heat the oil in a frying pan.
Stir fry the meat in small batches.
Remove from pan and set aside.
Add the shallots and garlic to the pan.
Cook until the shallots begin to soften.
Stir the mushrooms and cook for about 5 minutes, or until soft.
Remove the pan from the fire, stir in the flour (this prevents the flour all going lumpy).
Cook for a minute.
Stir constantly.
Add the tomato puree, the mustard, stock or water.
Bring the sauce to boil until it thickens.
Keep stirring otherwise the sauce will get all lumpy!
Add the beef to the pan and cook until piping hot.
Stir in the sour cream or crème fraîche.
Add pepper and salt to taste.
Garnish with parsley and serve with mashed potato or rice.

chilli con carne

450g minced steak
1 onion, chopped
2 cans tomatoes
Chilli powder to taste
Salt to taste
Dash of Worcestershire sauce
1 can of red kidney beans

In a pan brown the meat.
Drain the fat.
Add the chilli powder, salt and the tomatoes and the onion.
Add drained, washed kidney beans.
Add salt to taste.
Simmer for 30 to 45 minutes.
Serve with rice and a salad or as jacket potato filling.

chunky beef casserole

450g diced beef
2 carrots
2 potatoes
2 parsnips
1 onion, finely chopped
1 clove garlic, crushed
1 can chopped tomatoes
1 beef stock cube
500 ml water
1 tbsp olive oil

Peel the potatoes, parsnips and carrots and chop into small chunks.
Season some plain flour with salt and freshly ground black pepper.
Lightly coat the diced beef.
Brown the beef in one tablespoon olive oil and set aside.
Fry the onion until soft.
Add the garlic.
Return the beef to the saucepan.
Add the chopped vegetables and chopped tomatoes to the pan.
Pour over 500ml beef stock, made with one beef stock cube.
Cover and cook over a low heat for approximately 2 hours 30 minutes.
Serve in bowls with a slice of crusty French bread on the side.

cottage pie

450g minced beef
2 medium sized onions, chopped
1 level tbsp flour
½ tsp mixed herbs
½ tsp ground cinnamon
1 tbsp fresh chopped parsley
275 ml hot beef stock
1 tbsp tomato puree
A handful of cooked peas
Salt to taste
1 tbsp oil
Freshly ground pepper

topping

600g potatoes
50g butter
Salt and pepper to taste
25g grated cheese
Optional: crushed potato crisps

Preheat oven to 180 degrees C.
Heat the oil in a pan and fry the onions until soft.
Add the meat and cook for about 10 minutes.
Add pepper and salt to taste.
Add the cinnamon, mixed herbs, parsley and the cooked peas.
Stir in the flour mixed with the tomato puree and the hot stock.
Add to the meat and cook for 4 to 5 minutes.

topping

Boil and mash the potatoes with butter and add the grated cheese.
Put the meat mixture into an ovenproof dish.
Spread the potato mixture on top.
Sprinkle with a little crushed potato crisps.
Bake for 25 minutes or until the topping is nicely browned.

Peas can be substituted with carrots or mushrooms.

hamburgers / meatballs

400g lean minced beef or chicken
75g bacon (optional)
Salt to taste
Pinch of paprika
1 egg
Freshly ground pepper

Place the meat in a bowl, and the rest of the ingredients and mix well.
Divide into 4, shape into a ball; flatten it into a hamburger.
Grill and serve in hamburger buns.

meatballs

Make into 12 balls.
Serve this with any potato dish and a salad.

meatball sauce

250 ml tomato sauce
2 tsp hot chilli sauce
300 grape jam

Heat the tomato sauce and jelly in a pan, stirring constantly until the jam is melted.
Add the meatballs and stir until thoroughly coated.
Simmer uncovered for 30 minutes.

meatloaf
....

2 eggs
½ cup milk
2/3 cup bread crumbs
6 tbsp chopped onion
¼ tsp sage
Pepper and salt to taste
450g minced beef
½ cup tomato ketchup
3-4 tbsp brown sugar
½ tsp Worcestershire sauce

Preheat oven to 180 degrees C.
In a bowl, whisk the egg.
Add the milk and breadcrumbs, onion, salt, sage and pepper.
Add the beef and mix well.
Place in a loaf tin.
Combine the ketchup, brown sugar and Worcestershire sauce, spoon over the meat loaf.
Bake for 35 to 40 minutes or until the meat is no longer pink.
Slice and serve.

sloppy joe

450g minced beef
½ cup chopped onions
200g chopped tomatoes
½ cup water
2 tbsp oats
1-1½ tsp chilli powder
1-1½ tsp Worcestershire sauce
1 clove garlic, crushed
Dash of Tabasco or hot pepper sauce

Heat 1 tbsp oil in a pan and cook the meat and onions.
Add the water and the rest of the ingredients and cook well.
Serve with hamburger buns and a salad.

steak and kidney pie

450g steak, cubed
250g kidneys, cubed
1 medium onion
A dash of Worcestershire sauce
Salt to taste
Freshly ground pepper
2 level tbsp flour
A little oil
Short crust pastry or puff pastry

Heat oil in a pan, cook the chopped onion, cubed steak, kidney and brown.
Add the seasoned flour and a little water and cook the steak and kidney until tender.
Preheat oven to 180 degrees C.
Divide the pastry into two.
Line a pie dish with one half of the pastry.
Pour in the steak and kidney mixture.
Cover the top with the other piece of pastry.
Prick with a fork and make a few holes for the air to circulate.
Bake in the oven for 25 to 30 minutes until the pastry is cooked.

chicken

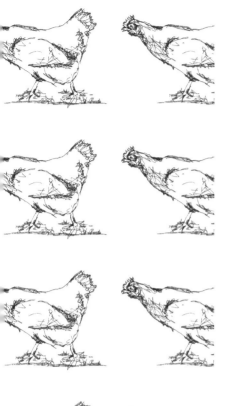

chicken with almonds
chicken cacciatore
chicken nuggets
chicken parmigina
chicken satay
chicken teriyaki
chicken tortilla pie
chicken wings with peanut sauce
chicken with banana peppers
cinnamon and honey chicken
crackling chicken with spinach
ginger and garlic chicken
hot pepper chicken
hunters chicken
lemon chicken
mediterranean chicken tart
soy roast chicken
spicy mango chicken
spicy yogurt chicken
Sri Lankan roast chicken
sweet and sour chicken

chicken with almonds

4 chicken breasts
1 tsp salt
1 tbsp corn flour
1 egg white
1½ tbsp rice wine
Oil for deep frying
125g green beans
1 medium onion
4 stalks celery
1 red pepper
125g mushrooms
185g water chestnuts
6 shallots or 6 spring onions
60g toasted almonds
2 tablespoons oil

sauce

1 tbsp corn flour
1 cup water
1 tbsp soy sauce
1 chicken stock cube
1 tbsp oyster sauce
1 tbsp rice wine
1 tbsp tomato sauce

To make the sauce, blend the corn flour with water and soy sauce.
Add crumbled stock cube, oyster sauce, tomato sauce and rice wine.
Stir over heat until sauce boils and thickens.

Cut the chicken breasts into strips.
Combine the salt, corn flour, lightly beaten egg white and the 1 ½ tablespoon rice wine in a bowl and mix well.
Coat the chicken breast pieces in this mixture.
Deep fry the chicken pieces in hot oil until cooked through and the drain.
Cut the beans, celery and pepper into strips.
Dice the onion.
Slice the mushrooms.
Drain water chestnuts, and cut in half.
Heat a little extra oil in a wok.
Add the vegetables, sauté until tender but crisp.
Add the chicken and heat thoroughly.
Pour the sauce over the chicken.
Sprinkle the toasted almonds.
Garnish with chopped spring onions.

chicken cacciatore

4 chicken thighs and legs
1 large onion
2 large carrots
2 celery stalks
2 tbsp white wine
400g chopped tomatoes
Salt and pepper to taste
50g stoned green olives
1 tbsp fresh rosemary leaves
2 tbsp olive oil

Peel and chop the onion.
Wash, trim and cut the carrots and the celery.
Heat olive oil in a large pan.
Sauté the chicken until browned.
Remove from pan.
Cook the onions for about 5 minutes.
Add the carrots and celery and sauté for 3 minutes.
Stir in the wine and the chopped tomatoes.
Add pepper and salt to taste.
Return the chicken to the pan.
Cover and simmer for about 15 minutes.
Add olives and rosemary.
Increase heat slightly and cook for another 10 minutes or until the chicken is tender.

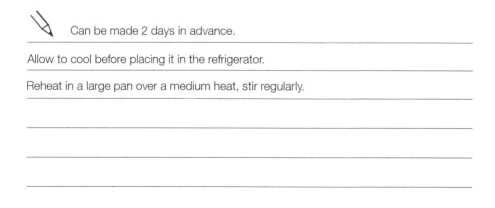

Can be made 2 days in advance.

Allow to cool before placing it in the refrigerator.

Reheat in a large pan over a medium heat, stir regularly.

chicken nuggets

2 chicken breasts
Black pepper
½ tsp Cajun spice or ½ tsp cayenne pepper
Breadcrumbs
Oil for frying

Wash and cut the chicken breasts into strips.
Mix the spices with the breadcrumbs.
Roll the chicken pieces in breadcrumbs.
Deep fry the nuggets until golden brown.

chicken parmigina

3 skinless chicken breasts
½ cup breadcrumbs
½ cup grated Parmesan cheese
1 egg
¼ cup olive oil
1 clove garlic crushed
1 tsp oregano
200g Mozzarella cheese
450g spaghetti sauce or freshly made tomato sauce

Preheat oven 180 degrees C.
Cut each breast into two or three pieces.
Combine breadcrumbs and ¼ cup Parmesan cheese in a shallow bowl.
In a separate bowl, whisk the egg.
Dip chicken in egg.
Then dip chicken in breadcrumbs coat thoroughly.
Repeat until all pieces are coated.
In a large frying pan heat ¼ cup of olive oil over medium heat, until hot.
Add chicken a few pieces at a time, sauté 5 minutes on each side turning once until golden brown.
Remove to plate repeat until all the chicken is done adding more oil if needed.
In a bowl combine spaghetti sauce and garlic and oregano or tarragon.
Place the chicken pieces in an oven proof dish.
Pour the sauce over the chicken.
Cover loosely with aluminium foil.
Bake for 40 minutes.
Remove the foil.
Place the mozzarella cheese over the chicken.
Sprinkle the remaining parmesan cheese.
Bake for another 10 minutes.

chicken satay

quick satay sauce

1 tbsp vegetable oil
½ tsp grated lemon rind
1 small onion
200 ml coconut cream
1 clove garlic
4 tbsp crunchy peanut butter
1cm piece ginger
1 tbsp soy sauce
1 kaffir lime leaf
1 tbsp sweet chilli sauce
1 red chilli, deseeded
Juice of ½ a lemon
¼ tsp chilli powder
1 tsp fish sauce
½ tsp turmeric powder
1 tbsp soft brown sugar
½ tsp cumin powder
200 ml hot water

Finely chop the onion, garlic, ginger, kaffir lime leaf and red chilli.
Heat a small pan with vegetable oil.
Add all of the chopped ingredients, the chilli, turmeric powder and cumin powder.
Mix together.
Fry until softened.
Add grated lemon rind, coconut cream, peanut butter, soy sauce and sweet chilli sauce.
Stir until smooth.
Now stir in the lemon juice, fish sauce, brown sugar and hot water.
Bring to a gentle boil.
Leave to simmer until the sauce thickens.

If you don't want to use ready made peanut butter, you can use 1 cup of raw peanuts – you need to fry these first, leave to cool and rub the skins off and discard this. Then pound the peanuts to form a fine paste. Use this in the above recipe instead of the peanut butter. // If the sauce looks a little too pale you can add more Soy sauce to darken the colour, but be careful not to make it too salty when you do this. // If you leave the sauce to go cold, it may go slightly darker brown on top – don't worry this will be fine if you just stir it up. You can warm this sauce up in a microwave. It should be served at room temperature/warm not chilled.

chicken satay (continued)

marinade
1 tbsp honey
2 tsp sesame oil
4 tbsp soy sauce
1 tsp turmeric
1 tsp coriander powder
½ tsp chilli powder

Make the chicken marinade by mixing the honey, soy sauce, sesame oil, ground coriander and turmeric, and the chilli powder together.

garnish
½ a cucumber
2 red onions

satay
Cut the chicken breast meat into thin slices lengthways.
Thread these onto wooden skewers.
Soak the chicken skewers in this marinade for at least 2 hours (or overnight in the refrigerator is the best).
To cook the chicken, place the skewers under a pre-heated grill for 5-10 minutes.
Baste the satay sticks with the remaining marinade throughout the cooking time.
Serve the chicken satay with a side dish of coarsely diced cucumber pieces
Small raw red onions cut into chunks.

Soak wooden skewers in a shallow dish of hot boiling water – this will help to prevent the exposed wood from burning when under the grill.

Satay can also be cooked on a barbecue which gives a more authentic flavour – great in summer!

chicken teriyaki

300g boneless chicken legs
200 ml Teriyaki sauce
1 tbsp sesame seeds
Oil for frying

Fry the boneless chicken legs till golden brown.
Add the chicken to the Teriyaki sauce.
Continue cooking until the meat absorbs the sauce.
Slice the chicken.
Sprinkle with sesame seeds and serve.

teriyaki sauce

500 ml water
50 ml sake or white wine
500g sugar
1 cm piece ginger, finely chopped
10g corn starch

Mix all the ingredients in a saucepan.
Bring to boil and reduce the sauce.
Add corn starch to thicken the sauce.

chicken tortilla pie

....

3 chicken breasts, boiled and shredded
Sweet corn kernels
6-8 tortillas, broken into small pieces
Pepper and salt to taste
1 can mushroom and chicken soup
Grated cheese to taste
A little chicken stock from the boiled chicken
Dash of cayenne pepper

Preheat oven to 170 degrees C.
Mix all the ingredients together reserving a little cheese for the top.
Add ¼ -½ cup chicken stock.
Put the mixture into an oven proof dish.
Top with a little cheese and a sprinkling of cayenne pepper.
Bake for 30-40 minutes.

chicken wings with peanut sauce

1 kg chicken wings
2 cloves garlic, crushed
1 tbsp brown sugar
½ tsp paprika
Pinch of dry chilli flakes
Pepper and salt to taste
Coriander leaves
Cucumber cut into chunks
Lime wedges

sauce

25g creamed coconut
3 tbsp crunchy peanut butter
1 tbsp light soy sauce
2 tbsp sweet chilli sauce

Preheat oven to 190 degrees C.
Cut the chicken wings between the joints.
Discard the tips or make a chicken stock with them.
Place the garlic, paprika, chilli flakes and pepper in a bowl.
Coat the chicken wings.
Bake for 35-45 minutes until golden brown.

garnish

Cucumber chunks
Coriander leaves

Dissolve the coconut cream in a pan with 200ml boiling water.
Stir until smooth.
Add the peanut butter, soy sauce and sweet chilli sauce.
Mix well and warm the sauce through.
Pile the wings on a plate and garnish with coriander leaves, cucumber chunks.
Serve the sauce separately.

It can be served as a starter or as a main meal with a bowl of rice.

chicken with banana peppers

1 kg chicken
2 tbsp oil
50g ginger finely chopped
4-8 green chillies
2 tsp soy sauce
10 cloves garlic, finely chopped
Salt to taste
250g banana peppers
250g pineapple cut into pieces

Cut, wash and drain chicken.
Heat the oil in a pan.
Cook the ginger, garlic and green chillies.
Add the chicken pieces, soy sauce and salt.
Keep frying the chicken over low heat till it browns.
Add the banana peppers and cook for about 10 minutes.
Add the pineapple pieces just before serving.

cinnamon and honey chicken

½ cup flour
2 tsp salt
¾ tsp cinnamon powder
¼ tsp turmeric powder
¼ tsp pepper powder
1 egg
6 pieces chicken thigh and leg
1/3 cup breadcrumbs
2 tbsp oil
¼ cup melted butter
¼ cup honey
1 tbsp lemon juice
2 tbsp milk

Preheat oven to 190 degrees C.
Mix together the flour, salt, cinnamon, turmeric and pepper.
Coat the chicken pieces with the flour mixture.
Whisk the egg and milk together.
Combine the whisked egg and milk with the breadcrumbs to form a soft moist mixture.
Roll the chicken pieces in the breadcrumb mixture.
Arrange on a wired baking tray.
Drizzle a little oil and bake for 30 minutes or until crisp and brown.
Mix together the butter, honey and lemon juice and pour over chicken.
Bake for another 15 minutes.
Remove from oven and serve immediately.

crackling chicken with spinach

1 bunch spinach, chopped
3 boneless chicken breasts
Oil for frying
4 red chillies, chopped
5g white sesame seeds, roasted
3 cloves garlic, crushed garlic
Salt to taste
1 egg white
20g corn starch
100 ml honey
1 tbsp Worcestershire sauce
1 tsp sesame oil

Heat the oil in a pan.
Place the spinach in a colander.
Dip into the hot oil and cook for 3- 4 seconds.
Remove and drain on a paper towel.
Heat the oil in a wok.
Cut the chicken into small pieces.
Season the chicken with salt.
Roll it in egg white, then in corn starch and deep fry in hot oil.
Make the sauce with the honey, Worcestershire sauce, crushed garlic and the chillies.
Mix thoroughly.
Coat the chicken with the sauce.
Sprinkle with sesame oil and sesame seeds.
Serve at once with the spinach.

ginger and garlic chicken

4 skinless, boneless chicken breasts
2 tbsp oil
2 cm pieces fresh ginger, finely chopped
1 tbsp soy sauce
1 onion, finely chopped
2 cloves garlic, crushed
Salt and pepper to taste
25 ml chicken stock

garnish

Spring onions
Chopped red peppers

Heat the oil in a wok.
Add the chicken breasts.
Cook until the meat is browned about 5 minutes.
Season with salt and pepper, add garlic and onions.
Cook for 1-2 minutes.
Add the soy sauce and the chicken stock.
Cover the wok with a lid and simmer for 10 minutes.
Stir occasionally.
Add the chopped ginger and cook for another 3 minutes.
Serve with boiled rice garnished with chopped red peppers and spring onions.

hot pepper chicken

300g boneless chicken
Salt to taste
Pinch of sugar
1 egg yolk
20g corn flour
30 ml cooking oil
1 tsp garlic chopped
½ tsp black pepper
½ -1 tsp red chillies
½ tsp butter
Few drops of chilli oil
Spring onions
Chopped coriander leaves
10 ml rice wine

Mix together the salt, sugar, egg yolk and corn flour.
Marinate the chicken pieces for 30 minutes.
Heat oil in a pan and deep fry the chicken.
Set aside.
Heat a little more oil in a wok.
Add the garlic, black pepper, chilli and butter.
Cook for 2 minutes.
Add the chicken, chilli oil, spring onions, coriander leaves and rice wine.
Toss well.

hunter's chicken

1 tablespoon vegetable oil
4 chicken breasts on the bone
1 teaspoon salt
½ tsp freshly ground black pepper
1 tbsp butter
1 onion, chopped
300g mushrooms, sliced
2 cloves garlic, minced
1 tbsp flour
½ cup white wine
2/3 cup chicken stock
1 cup chopped tomatoes
¼ tsp dried thyme
¼ tsp rosemary

In a large, skillet, heat the oil on medium to high heat.
Season chicken with quarter teaspoon of the salt and pepper, and add to the hot pan.
Cook until browned, about 10 minutes.
Remove chicken and reserve.
Pour off all but a tablespoon of the oil from the pan.
Add butter to the pan and reduce the heat to medium-low.
Add the onion and cook until softened, about 5 minutes.
Raise heat to medium-high, and add the mushrooms.
Cook stirring occasionally until the mushrooms are browned, about 5 minutes.
Add flour and garlic, and cook for 1 minute.
Stir in the white wine, and bring to a simmer.
Add the stock, tomatoes, thyme, rosemary, pepper, and the remaining salt.
Add the reserved chicken and any juices.
Reduce heat to medium-low and simmer, covered, until the chicken is done, about 10-12 minutes.

lemon chicken

1 tsp white sesame seeds
1½ cups cornstarch
3 cups peanut or vegetable oil
1 tbsp oil for stir frying
Lemon slices
400g skinless boneless chicken breasts
or thighs cut in to cubes

marinade

1 tbsp soy sauce
1 tsp sesame oil
2 large egg whites
2 garlic cloves, minced
½ tbsp minced ginger
¼ cup chicken stock
3 tbsp fresh lemon juice
2 tsp grated lemon zest
1 tbsp soy sauce
2 tbsp sugar
1 tsp cornstarch, dissolved in 1 tbsp water

In a bowl combine the soy sauce, sesame oil, and egg whites.
Add the chicken and stir gently to coat.
Let it stand at room temperature for 10 minutes.
Toast the sesame seeds in a dry pan for about a minute.
Transfer to a dish and set aside.
Coat the chicken pieces with cornstarch.
Heat the oil in a wok or a deep pan.
Fry the chicken pieces until golden brown.
Remove chicken, drain and set aside.

sauce

Heat 1 tablespoon of oil in a wok or a small pan.
Add the garlic and ginger and cook until fragrant, about 30 seconds.
Add the chicken stock, lemon juice, lemon zest, soy sauce, and sugar.
Stir until the sugar is dissolved.
Simmer the sauce until it is reduced by half.
Stir in the cornstarch mixture to thicken the sauce.
Remove from the heat and toss the fried chicken in the sauce.
Transfer to a serving dish and garnish with the toasted sesame seeds and lemon slices.

mediterranean chicken tart

500g short crust pastry
1 tbsp olive oil
2 chicken breasts, thinly sliced
A few springs of fresh thyme
2 cloves garlic, crushed
3 eggs
300g natural yogurt
25g Parmesan cheese, grated
Salt and pepper to taste
50g black and green olives
6 sundried tomatoes in oil, chopped
Mixed peppers, deseeded and quartered

Preheat oven to 200 degrees C.
Roll out pastry and line a 23 cm flan dish.
Heat a little oil in a frying pan.
Add the chicken, thyme and garlic and cook for 5-6 minutes.
Take the thyme out.
Preheat a grill.
Place the peppers skin side uppermost, under the grill until the skins begin to blacken.
Remove and cool.
Peel the skin and slice into strips.
Combine the chicken with the peppers, eggs, yogurt and Parmesan cheese.
Add seasoning to taste.
Spoon into the pastry case.
Arrange the olives and sundried tomatoes on top.
Bake in preheated oven for 30-40 minutes or until golden brown.
Cool slightly before serving.

soy roast chicken

1kg chicken
1 tbsp soy sauce
Freshly ground pepper
A little honey
1 tsp 5 spices powder

Preheat oven to 190 degrees C.
Mix the soy sauce, pepper and 5 spices powder.
Coat the chicken well and roast as per the weight.
Just before chicken is done, coat with honey.
Put it back in the oven for a few minutes for the skin to crisp and turn a golden brown in colour.

spicy mango chicken

2 red onions, sliced
3 cardamom pods, crushed
2 cloves garlic, crushed
2.5 cm fresh ginger, grated
2 half ripe mangoes
25g butter
5 cm stick cinnamon
¼ tsp ground coriander
½ tsp ground cumin
250g natural yogurt
Salt and pepper
3 cloves
Chopped fresh coriander
500g chicken breasts

Peel and cut the mangoes into thin slices.
Melt the butter in the pan.
Add the chicken and cook for 4-5 minutes or until the chicken is browned.
Add the garlic.
 Fry for one minute.
Add the cardamom pods, cloves and cinnamon and fry for another minute.
Add the onions and cook for 5 minutes, stir frequently.
Add the mango, ginger, ground coriander and cumin.
Cook over a low heat for 5 minutes.
Stir occasionally.
Add the yogurt, heat through gently.
Do not boil.
Add pepper and salt to taste.
Garnish with fresh chopped coriander and serve at once.

spicy yogurt chicken

8 skinless chicken drumsticks
145 ml yogurt
½ tsp chilli powder
1 tbsp cumin powder
1 tbsp coriander powder
2 tsp turmeric powder

Make a few slashes on each drumstick.
Mix all the ingredients.
Rub it well into the meat.
Cover and chill for at least 30 minutes.
Remove the drumsticks from the marinade.
Cook on barbeque or grill for 20-25 minutes until cooked through.

Sri Lankan roast chicken

1½ kg chicken
3 cloves of garlic
1 cm piece of ginger
¼ tsp freshly ground pepper
½ tsp salt
¼ tsp cinnamon powder
¼ tsp turmeric powder
Pinch of ground cloves
25 ml vinegar
50g butter

Preheat oven to 190 degrees C.
Wash and dry the chicken.
Crush garlic, ginger, pepper, salt and combine with cinnamon, turmeric, cloves,
vinegar and butter.
Rub this mixture all over the chicken and allow to stand for 30 minutes.
Place the chicken in a roasting tray together with the marinade and roast for 1½ hours.
Baste occasionally while roasting.

sweet and sour chicken

250g chicken breast, cut into pieces
1 onion, quartered
1 piece pineapple, cubed
1 green pepper, sliced
1 tablespoon oil

batter

2 tbsp flour
A little milk
1 egg

Whisk the egg with the milk.
Dip the chicken in the milk and egg mixture.
Coat the chicken with the flour.
Deep fry the chicken pieces.
Remove and drain.
Heat one tablespoon of oil in a wok.
Quickly stir fry the onion, green pepper and pineapple.
Remove and place in a dish along with the chicken.
Pour the sweet and sour sauce over it and serve.

sweet and sour sauce

1 tbsp corn flour
2 tsp soya sauce
2 tbsp vinegar
2 tbsp sugar
250 ml chicken stock
125 ml pineapple juice
A little paprika

Blend all the ingredients and boil for 2-3 minutes, until transparent.

Alternatively use chip shop batter mix.

Substitute chicken with pork

duck

crispy Sichuan duck
duck omelette
roast duck with orange sauce
sweet chilli duck breast

crispy Sichuan duck

1 ½ kg duck
2 tsp salt
3 thin slices of ginger
3 spring onions
3 tbsp rice wine
4 star anise
2 tsp Sichuan pepper or black pepper
1 tsp 5 spice powder
Oil for frying

to serve

Thin pancakes
Hoisin sauce or plum sauce
6 spring onions cut into thin strips
Cucumber cut into thin strips

Clean the duck well. Rub with salt.
Mix ginger, spring onions, rice wine, five spice powder, star anise and peppercorns and marinate the duck overnight.
Turn the duck over several times.
Place duck with the marinade in a deep dish in a steamer and steam for at least 3 hours. If you do not have a large enough steamer, transfer the duck to a saucepan with 1 ½ litres of stock and simmer gently for 3 hours.
Remove the duck, drain.
Remove and discard the spices.
Let a duck cool a little.
Heat oil in a wok or deep-fryer and fry the duck for 12 – 15 minutes over a medium heat until the skin is brown and crispy.
Remove the duck and drain oil.
To serve pull the meat off the bone and wrap it in the pancakes with the strips of spring onions, cucumber and the hoisin or plum sauce.

Thin pancakes can be bought at Chinese grocery stores.

duck omelette

¼ cup oil
½-1 tsp sesame oil
2 duck legs
1 tbsp grated ginger
6 dried shitake mushrooms
2 tbsp oil
6 eggs
2 tsp soy sauce
1 handful bean sprouts
Spring onions, finely sliced

Preheat oven to 180 degrees C.
Roast duck legs for 15-20 minutes.
Cool slightly and take the meat off the bone.
Finely slice the duck meat.
In a frying pan, heat the oil and sesame oil.
Add the duck, ginger and shitake mushrooms and sauté for a few minutes.
Remove ingredients from the pan.
Wipe the pan clean.
In a bowl, lightly whisk the eggs with the soy sauce.
Heat the pan and pour in the eggs and swirl it around.
Allow to set and cook for a few minutes.
Add the duck mixture and bean sprouts to one side and fold the omelette in half.

roast duck with orange sauce

1.75 - 2.25 kg duck
Salt

garnish

Orange slices
Watercress sprigs

sauce

1 onion, finely chopped
1 tbsp oil
25 g plain flour
150 ml orange juice
2 tbsp brandy
Salt and pepper

Preheat oven to 190 degrees C.
Calculate cooking time.
Allow 30 minutes per 450g.
Rub the salt over the duck.
Place the duck on a wire rack in a roasting tin and roast for the calculated time.
Remove the duck from the oven and place on a hot serving dish to keep warm.
Pour off the fat and reserve any juices from the tin.

sauce

Fry the onion in oil until soft.
Add the flour and gradually blend in the orange juice, stock and reserved juices.
Bring the sauce to the boil, reduce the heat and simmer gently for 2 minutes.
Add the brandy and seasoning.
Serve the duck garnished with orange slices and watercress.
Serve the sauce separately.

sweet chilli duck breast

4 duck breasts

marinade
½ cup sweet chilli sauce
½ cup soy sauce
Zest of 1 lime
Juice of 1 lime
1 red chilli thinly sliced

Combine sweet chilli sauce, soy sauce, lime zest and juice together in a large glass bowl.
Place the duck breasts in the marinade with the skin side up.
Cover and marinate for 24 hours in the refrigerator.
Preheat grill or the barbeque.
Score duck breast skin 4-5 times lightly with a sharp knife.
Grill the duck breasts for 5-6 minutes.
Baste the duck with the marinade.
Turn it over and crisp the skin.
Remove from grill and rest the duck for 3-4 minutes.
Serve the duck thinly sliced with grilled vegetables, a wedge of lime and a little sweet
chilli sauce and sliced fresh chilli.

lamb

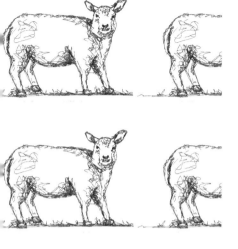

chilli lemon lamb cutlets
grilled lamb with feta cheese and lemon
lamb burgers
lamb shanks
lamb shanks with chickpeas
lamb stew
pistachio crumbed lamb cutlets
Sri Lankan roast lamb

chilli lemon lamb cutlets

8 lamb cutlets
1 lemon, halved
2 tbsp yogurt
Few drops of Tabasco sauce
2 cloves garlic, crushed
2 tsp chopped coriander leaves

Put the lamb cutlets in a bowl and squeeze half a lemon over them.
Add the rest of the ingredients and mix well.
Grill or cook lamb cutlets in a large frying pan.

grilled lamb with feta cheese and lemon

6-8 lamb cutlets
1 block feta cheese
Salt and pepper to taste
Juice of 1 lemon
Fresh oregano springs
Fresh thyme sprigs
Oil for frying and drizzling

Strip the leaves off the oregano and thyme sprigs.
Place in a bowl and drizzle with a little oil.
Crumble the feta cheese.
Add the salt and pepper and lemon juice and mix thoroughly.
Heat a pan until hot.
Brush each cutlet with a little oil and place in the hot pan.
Cook for a few minutes each side until cooked.
Transfer the cooked cutlets on to a serving dish.
Gently pour over the feta and herb dressing.

lamb burgers

500g lamb mince
1 tsp mustard
Pepper and salt to taste
Burger buns
Zest of 1 lemon
Freshly made breadcrumbs

Preheat the oven to 180 degrees C.
In a blender, whizz two of the burger buns to make breadcrumbs.
In a bowl, combine the breadcrumbs, lamb mince, lemon zest, mustard and a generous pinch of salt and pepper.
Shape into five burger patties and chill for at least 30 minutes.
Cook the burgers for 4 minutes on each side, until cooked thoroughly.
Lightly toast the bread rolls pop the hamburger in.

lamb shanks
....

3 lean lamb shanks
1 tbsp oil
2 garlic cloves, peeled and crushed
1 onion, peeled and chopped
1 carrot, peeled and chopped
2 celery stalks, sliced
2 tbsp horseradish sauce
400g tomato passata
Salt and pepper to taste
300 ml hot lamb stock
2 fresh rosemary stalks
450g baby potatoes, scrubbed

Preheat the oven to 150 degrees C.
Heat the oil in a large frying pan.
Add the lamb shanks and fry until browned approx 10 minutes.
Add the garlic, onion, carrot, celery, horseradish sauce and stir together.
Pour over the passata, stock and bring to a boil.
Add salt and pepper to taste.
Transfer to a casserole dish and add the rosemary.
Cover and cook in oven for 1½ hours.
Add the potatoes, making sure they are covered in the liquid.
Continue cooking for a further 30-45 minutes until potatoes are tender and the meat is falling from the bone.

lamb shanks with chickpeas

3 lean lamb shanks
1 tbsp oil
2 garlic cloves, crushed
6 shallots, peeled and left whole
150 ml red wine
400g chopped tomato
15 ml anchovy sauce or paste
1 sachet bouquet garni
Salt to taste
Freshly ground black pepper
250g can chickpeas drained

Preheat the oven to 160 degrees C.
Heat oil in a large pan and brown the lamb shanks for 6-8 minutes, turning occasionally.
Add the shallots, garlic and cook for 1-2 minutes.
Add the wine, chopped tomatoes, anchovy paste, herbs and seasoning.
Bring to the boil.
Transfer to an ovenproof casserole dish.
Cook for 2½-3 hours until the meat falls away from the bone.
Forty minutes before the end of the cooking time, add the chick peas.
Mix well, cover and return to the oven for the remaining cooking time.

lamb stew

1 kg lamb or mutton
1 tsp mustard
2 carrots
2 turnips or potatoes
2 leeks
1 cm piece of cinnamon
2 large onions
4 cloves garlic
10 peppercorns
1 tbsp Worcestershire sauce
Salt to taste
1 tbsp oil

Heat the oil in a pan and brown the meat.
Pour in sufficient boiling water to cover the meat.
Let it simmer very gently for about an hour.
Add the vegetables and seasoning and simmer until the meat is cooked.
If necessary thicken gravy with a little flour.

pistachio crumbed lamb cutlets

30g pistachio nuts, shelled and skinned
25g butter, melted
1 tbsp fresh thyme
1 tbsp fresh parsley
50g bread crumbs
Zest of ½ a lemon
1 tbsp oil
2 tsp Dijon mustard
8 lamb cutlets

Preheat the oven to 180 degrees C.
Place the nuts, melted butter, thyme and parsley in a food processor and blitz until finely chopped.
Add the breadcrumbs, lemon zest and season.
Blitz again.
Remove excess fat from the lamb cutlets.
Heat a frying pan until very hot add a teaspoon of olive oil.
Put the lamb cutlets in the pan and sear both sides.
Remove and transfer to a roasting tin.
Brush each side of the cutlet with mustard.
Sprinkle roughly one tablespoon of the crumb mixture onto each side.
Drizzle a little olive oil.
Roast for 5-8 minutes until the crust is golden and the lamb tender.

To skin pistachios pour hot water over the nuts which helps the skin to comes off easily.

Sri Lankan roast lamb

2 kg leg of lamb
1 tbsp cumin seeds
2 tsp coriander seeds
2 tsp fennel seeds
2 tsp black peppercorns
4 cloves of garlic
2 green chillies, finely chopped
330ml curd or Greek yoghurt
4 onions, peeled and thinly sliced

In a wok or pan dry roast the cumin, fennel and coriander seeds.
Remove from wok, add the pepper and grind to a powder.
In a pestle and mortar, grind the garlic and chillies with a little salt. Mix the ground spices and the garlic and chillies with the yogurt.
Make small incisions with a knife on the leg of lamb.
Pour the yogurt mixture and coat the leg of lamb well.
Cover and leave to marinade overnight or at least 8 hours.
Preheat oven to 200 degrees C.
Line a baking tray with foil.
Arrange the thinly sliced onions on the foil.
Place the lamb on top of the onions.
Wrap the lamb with foil.
Cook in oven for 90 minutes.
Open the foil and cook for a further 30 minutes.

serve

Pile some pilau rice on a flat oval dish.
Place the lamb in the middle, sprinkle with chopped coriander leaves.

pork

baked spare ribs
chinese roast pork
coffee ribs
italian style pork
pork dumplings
pork and prawn stir fry
pork with spinach and coconut cream
pulled pork

baked pork spare ribs

1 tbsp oil
1/3 cup light soy sauce
8 pork spare ribs
2 tbsp lemon juice
½ tsp five spices powder
2 tsp fresh ginger grated
2 tbsp Hoisin sauce
2 cloves garlic crushed

Preheat oven to 160 degrees C.
Heat the oil in pan.
Add the ribs and cook until well browned all over.
Add the remaining ingredients, stir over heat until mixture boils.
Place ribs on a wire rack.
Reserve the sauce mix.
Bake ribs for about 50 minutes or until tender.
Brush with the reserved sauce mixture during cooking.

Chinese roast pork

1½ kg belly pork
1 tsp baking soda
1 tsp Chinese 5 spices powder
Light soy sauce
Salt
Rice wine

Wash belly pork.
Boil a pan of water and cook the belly for 10 minutes.
Take out and dry well.
Punch holes on the skin and dry with paper towels.
Coat the skin with the baking soda and a pinch of salt.
Mix the 5 spices powder with the soy sauce and rice wine in a dish.
Place the meat with the skin side up in the marinade and marinate for 12 hours.
Do not cover the meat – it needs to be air dried in the refrigerator.
Preheat oven to 230 degrees C.
Punch holes again on the skin.
Dry with paper towels and remove all moisture.
Cover skin with 2.5 cm thick of salt.
Fill a pan one third with water and place in the bottom shelf of the oven.
Place the pork on a wire rack.
While the pork is cooking the fat will drip into the pan with water.
Bake for 30-40 minutes.
Take out and remove salt.
Bake again for another 10 minutes.
Reduce heat to 200 degrees C.
Bake for another 10 minutes.

coffee ribs

....

8 pieces pork ribs
2 egg whites
Salt to taste
3 tbsp corn starch
Vegetable oil, for deep frying
1 tbsp instant coffee
1 tsp sugar
2 tsp milk powder
3 tbsp oyster sauce
1 red chillies, sliced
1 tbsp sugar
2 spring onions, sliced
3 tbsp cornstarch
2 tsp ground cinnamon, for dusting

Rub the egg whites and salt onto the ribs and marinate for 20 minutes.
Then rub in the cornstarch into the ribs.
Allow to sit for 10 minutes.
Heat the oil in a wok.
Deep fry the ribs for about 5 minutes.
Remove from the heat and set aside.
In a large frying pan mix the ½ cup of water, the instant coffee, 1 teaspoon sugar and 2 teaspoon milk powder.
Place over medium heat.
Add the oyster sauce, the chilli and salt.
When it starts to simmer, add one tablespoon sugar and allow the sauce to caramelise.
Add the ribs to the sauce and toss to evenly coat.
Place the ribs in a serving dish and top with spring onions and cinnamon.

To test whether the oil is hot, insert a chopstick, if bubbles form around the

chopstick the oil is ready.

Italian style pork chops

4 lean pork chops
1 tablespoon olive oil
1 onion, finely chopped
2 cloves garlic, crushed
1 tbsp chopped fresh rosemary
1 tbsp grated lemon rind
¼ tsp crushed dried chillies
150 ml chicken stock
400g chopped tomatoes
Salt and pepper to taste

Trim the excess fat from the chops.
Make slits in the chops and place a few thin slices of garlic or lemon.
Heat the oil in a large frying pan.
Arrange the chops in a single layer and cook on each side for a couple of minutes.
Remove chops from pan and place on a plate.
Add the onions to the pan keep stirring and cook for 5 minutes.
Add the crushed garlic, chopped rosemary, grated lemon rind and crushed chillies and cook for 1 minute.
Reduce the heat to low, add the chops, stock and tomatoes to the onions.
Simmer for 10-15 minutes until the chops are cooked through and the sauce is thick.
Remove from fire, add salt and pepper.

pork and prawn dumplings

150g chicken
150g prawns
½ tsp sugar
1 tsp sesame oil
¼ tsp white pepper
Won ton skins
A little cornstarch
Salt to taste

Separate the won ton skins.
Mince chicken and prawns and mix with sugar, salt, sesame oil and cornstarch.
Place a little of the mixture on the centre of the won ton skin.
Wet the sides with a little water.
Gather the corners and make them into little parcels like a draw string purse.
Steam a few dumplings at a time in a steamer.

Replace pork with chicken (see also vegetarian dumplings)

pork and prawn stir fry

2 tbsp peanut oil
350g pork mince
300g uncooked prawns, shelled
3 garlic cloves, crushed
1 tbsp fresh ginger, grated
1 red chilli, chopped finely
3 eggs, beaten lightly
2 tsp soy sauce
1 tbsp tomato sauce
30 ml chilli garlic sauce
30 sweet chilli sauce
50 ml fish sauce
3 tbsp brown sugar
2 green onions, sliced thinly
300g bean sprouts
2 tbsp coriander, chopped finely

Combine, sauces and sugar in a pan.
Cook, stirring until the sugar dissolves.
Heat the oil in a wok.
Add the pork, garlic and ginger until pork is browned and almost cooked.
Add the prawns and chilli.
Cook until prawns turn pink, add the egg, stir fry until just set.
Add onions, bean sprouts and coriander, cook until sprouts are just tender.

pork with spinach and coconut cream

4 pork loin chops
1 kg sweet potato
1 clove garlic, chopped fine
1 red chilli, chopped fine
450g fresh spinach
1½ tbsp olive oil
150 ml coconut cream

Preheat oven to 200 degrees C.
Peel and cut sweet potato in thick rounds.
Coat with 1 tablespoon of oil.
Arrange the sweet potato in a single layer on a baking sheet.
Bake in the oven for 25 minutes or until golden.
Heat half tablespoon of oil in the frying pan.
Add the pork and cook for 3-4 minutes on each side.
Transfer to a plate and cover with foil to keep warm.
To the pan in which the pork has been cooked, add the garlic and chilli.
Cook for 30 seconds.
Add the spinach and coconut cream and cook.
Stir for 2 minutes or until the spinach just wilts.
Arrange the sweet potato on a flat dish.
Top with the spinach mixture.
Place the pork on to and serve.

pulled pork

2 onions, sliced
3 bay leaves
1 tbsp mustard powder
1 tbsp smoked paprika
140g tomato ketchup
4 tbsp red wine vinegar
1 tbsp Worcestershire sauce
3 tbsp soft dark brown sugar
1 tsp freshly ground black pepper
Salt to taste
1.5-2 kg pork shoulder, boned with rind attached and tied

Preheat oven to140 degrees C.
Place the onions and bay leaves in the bottom of a large roasting tin.
Mix mustard powder, paprika and 1 teaspoon ground black pepper with a pinch of salt.
Rub this mixture all over the pork including all the crevices.
Place the pork, rind-side up, on top of the onions.
Pour 200ml water into the bottom of the tin, wrap the pork with foil and bake for 4 hours.
In a bowl, mix the ketchup, vinegar, Worcestershire sauce and brown sugar.
Remove the pork from the tin and pat dry.
Place the roasting tin on the hob, pour in the ketchup mixture and let it bubble vigorously for 10-15 minutes until thick and glossy.
Remove the bay leaves and pour the sauce into a food processor and blitz until smooth.
Spread half the sauce mixture over the meat.
Heat the grill to high.
Place the pork on a baking tray and grill each side for 10-15 minutes until nicely charred.
Lift the pork onto a large plate or tray.
Remove string and peel off the skin.
Using 2 forks shred the meat into chunky pieces.
Add 3-4 tablespoons of the barbecue sauce to the meat and toss everything to coat.
Pile into bread rolls and serve with extra sauce and a little coleslaw.

Pork can be barbequed. Place the pork skin-side down on the grill. Cook for

15 minutes until nicely charred, then flip over and cook for another 10 minutes. The

meat will be very tender.

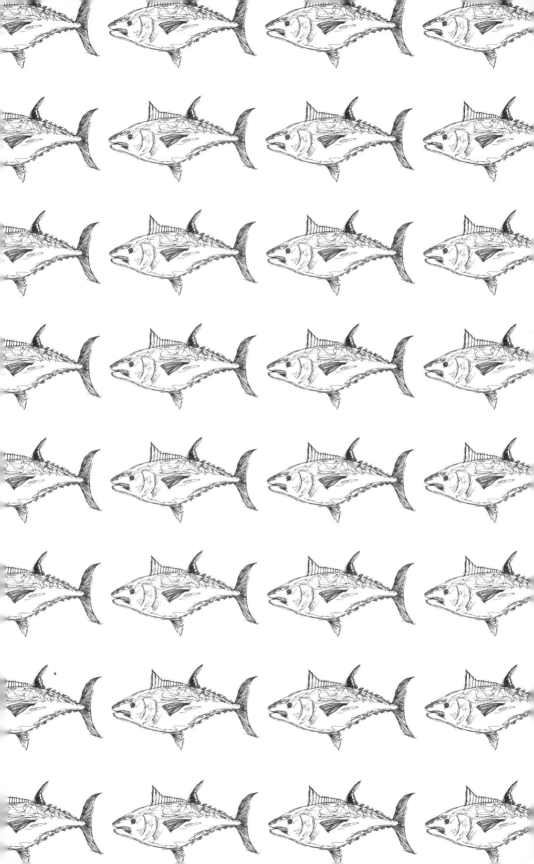

seafood

baked fish with thai spices
chilli fish
crispy squid
devilled prawns
fish baked in banana leaf
fish pie with cheese swirls
grilled fish with avocado salsa
lemon crusted baked fish
masala pomfret
mussels in wine
mussels stuffed with garlic
mussels with coriander cream
oriental salmon steaks
quick baked Asian fish
salmon fillet with a horseradish crust
steamed fish with garlic and ginger

baked fish with thai spices

4 trout fillets
1 stalk lemon grass, finely chopped
1 cm piece ginger, finely chopped
1 red chilli, deseeded and chopped
1 clove garlic, finely chopped
1 tbsp fish sauce
Juice of 2 lemons
1 tsp golden sugar
Coriander leaves, chopped

Preheat oven to 180 degrees C.
Oil a large sheet of foil.
Place the fillets skin side down in the centre of the sheet.
Make the sauce by mixing together the rest of ingredients.
Spoon half the mixture over the fillets.
Tightly wrap the foil and bake for 12-15 minutes.
Serve with the rest of the sauce.

chilli fish

....

4 fish fillets
2 tsp olive oil
2 tbsp honey
10 ml light soy sauce
1 red chilli, deseeded and finely chopped
2 tsp sesame oil
200g baby spinach leaves
2 tsp grated ginger
Lime wedges, to serve
Sea salt

Combine honey, soy sauce and chilli in a small bowl, and set aside.
Season the fish with sea salt.
In a frying pan heat 2 teaspoons olive oil and 1 teaspoon sesame oil.
Cook the fish skin side down for 5 minutes or until the skin crisps.
Turn and cook the fish for a further 2 minutes or until cooked through.
Heat remaining 2 teaspoons of olive oil and 1 teaspoon sesame oil in a wok over high heat.
Add the spinach and ginger, and stir-fry for 1 minute.
Layer a plate with spinach and place the fish on top.
Pour the chilli sauce over the fish.
Serve with wedges of lime.

crispy squid

250 ml oil
2 tbsp corn flour
4 tbsp semolina
1 tsp salt
1 tsp cayenne pepper
500g squid cut into rings

garlic mayonnaise
2 garlic clove, crushed
8 tbsp mayonnaise

Heat the oil in a wok or a deep pan.
Mix the semolina, corn flour and the seasoning in a freezer bag.
Add the squid rings to the bag and shake gently to coat the squid completely.
Fry the squid in batches for 2-3 minutes until golden and crisp.
Remove from the oil with a slotted spoon and drain on kitchen paper.
Stir the crushed garlic into the mayonnaise.
Serve the sauce on the side.

devilled prawns

1 kg prawns
1 large onion, slices
2 -3 banana peppers, cut diagonally
3 cloves garlic, minced
1 cm piece ginger, minced
¼ tsp turmeric powder
1 tbsp soy sauce
1 tbsp tomato ketchup
½ -2 tsp chilli powder
3 tbsp oil
Salt to taste

Shell and devein the prawns.
Heat the oil in a pan.
Fry the ginger garlic, turmeric powder and the chilli powder until fragrant.
Add the prawns and cook till it turns pink.
Do not overcook.
Add the remaining ingredients and cook until the onions are soft.
Serve hot.

fish baked in banana leaf

4 large fillets of white fish

marinade
½ tsp cumin
1 tsp coriander
1 tsp fennel
10-12 cloves garlic
1 tbsp red chilli powder
¼ tsp turmeric powder
4 tsp ghee
100g curd or yogurt
Juice of 1 lime
Salt to taste
A handful of chopped fresh coriander

Preheat oven to 170 degrees C.
In a small pan, dry roast the cumin, coriander and fennel and grind to a fine powder.
Next, roast the garlic and grind to a paste with a pinch of salt.
Combine the ground spices and garlic paste with the chilli powder, turmeric, salt, lime juice, curd and ghee.
Mix well.
Add in a handful of chopped coriander to the marinade.
Coat the fish with the marinade.
Leave for 20 minutes.
Place the fish on the banana leaf and fold over to make a parcel and tie with a string.
Bake in the oven for 20 minutes.

If you do not have a banana leaf, on a sheet of foil, place a greaseproof paper

and place the fish and make a parcel.

fish pie with cheese swirls

450g seer fish or any white fish
(boiled and flaked)
¾ cup fish stock
½ cup milk
1 tbsp tomato ketchup
1 tbsp flour
Salt and pepper to taste
1 small onion, chopped
100g green peas
3 carrots, cooked and diced
25g butter
1 lime
Crispy fried bacon (optional)
1-2 green chilli chopped finely
Chopped parsley

cheese swirls

300g flour
1 tsp baking powder
Salt to taste
120g butter
200g grated cheese
A little milk
2 well beaten eggs

Melt the butter, fry the onions and chilli, add the flour and cook.
Stir in the stock, milk, tomato ketchup, salt and pepper.
Cook till thick.
When cooked, add the lime juice.
Butter an oven proof dish.
Spread a layer of green peas, carrots, minced bacon and then the fish.
Pour sauce over it.
Sprinkle with chopped parsley and cover with cheese swirls.

cheese swirls

Mix flour, baking powder and salt in a bowl.
Rub in the butter and mix to a soft dough with a little milk.
Knead lightly.
Roll out on a floured board to 1cm thickness.
Mix cheese with the beaten egg and spread onto pastry and roll like a Swiss roll.
Dampen the edges to seal.
Wrap in cling film and leave in refrigerator for 20 minutes.
Cut into slices.
Place on top of fish.
Bake in a preheated oven at 170 degrees C for 20-30 minutes.

grilled fish with avocado salsa

1 pomfret
A little semolina
Oil to shallow fry

masala

2 tsp ginger
3 cloves garlic
1 tbsp oil
½ tbsp turmeric powder
1 tsp red chilli powder
Juice of 1 lime

Peel and chop the avocado into small chunks.
Chop the plum tomatoes into small chunks.
Finely slice the onion.
Chop the coriander leaves.
Gently mix all the ingredients except the fish and set aside.
Heat the pan until very hot.
Rub a little salt and pepper on the fish.
Drizzle with a little olive oil.
Cook the fillets for 2-3 minutes on each side until charred and cooked through.
Serve with avocado salsa and a salad.

lemon crusted baked fish

70g breadcrumbs
A little lemon juice
Freshly ground pepper
2 tbsp green pesto
50g green olives, chopped
1 tbsp olive oil
4 fillets of sea bass (or any other white fish)

Preheat oven to 190 degrees C.
In a mixing bowl mix the breadcrumbs, lemon and pepper with the pesto.
Add the chopped green olives.
Heat a pan with 1 tablespoon olive oil.
Place the fish fillets skin side down in the pan for 1-2 minutes to colour.
Remove from the heat and place on a baking tray skin side down.
Spoon the crumb mixture over each fillet to cover.
Bake until the fish is cooked through and the crust is golden brown in colour about 5–8 minutes.

masala pomfret

4 pomfret fillets
1 stalk lemon grass, finely chopped
1 cm piece ginger, finely chopped
1 red chilli, deseeded and chopped
1 clove garlic, finely chopped
1 tbsp fish sauce
Juice of 2 lemons
1 tsp golden sugar
Coriander leaves, chopped

Preheat oven to180 degrees C.
Oil a large sheet of foil.
Place the fillets skin side down in the centre of the sheet.
Make the sauce by mixing together the rest of ingredients.
Spoon half the mixture over the fillets.
Tightly wrap the foil and bake for 12-15 minutes.
Serve with the rest of the sauce.

mussels in wine

2 kg mussels in shells
2 cloves garlic, chopped
1 tbsp olive oil
2 shallots, chopped
200 ml white wine
Freshly ground pepper
1 bunch parsley, chopped
Fresh cream or crème fraîche (optional)

Clean mussels and scrape off the threads on the shells.
Rinse under cold running water.
If any are open discard them.
Heat the olive oil in a large pan and add the garlic and shallots.
Cook the onion and garlic for 5 minutes.
Do not let them brown.
Add the mussels and mix well.
Add the wine and cover the pan.
Increase the heat and cook for 3-4 minutes.
All the shells should be opened.
Discard those that have not opened.
Season to taste, add the cream, the chopped parsley and mix well.

garlic stuffed mussels

1 kg fresh mussels
150g butter
Pepper and salt to taste
25g fresh breadcrumbs
Lemon juice
1 tbsp fresh parsley, chopped
4 cloves garlic, crushed

Clean mussels and scrape off the threads on the shells.
Rinse under cold running water.
If any are open discard them.
Preheat the grill.
Place the mussels in a heavy based pan.
Cover with the tight fitting lid and cook over a high heat for 3 -4 minutes.
Shake the pan occasionally until the mussels have opened.
Discard any that do not open.
Remove the top shell from each of the mussels.
Arrange the shell with the mussel in an ovenproof dish.
In a small pan melt the butter.
Add the garlic, parsley and lemon juice.
Add the breadcrumbs and mix well.
Add pepper and salt to taste.
Place a little of the mixture on top of the mussels.
Place mussels under the grill for 3 – 5 minutes or until the breadcrumbs are golden brown.
Serve with lemon wedges.

mussels with coriander cream

2 kg mussels
1 tbsp of butter
1 red onion, finely chopped
4 cloves garlic, crushed
A little white wine
150 ml single cream
Coriander leaves, roughly chopped
Pepper and salt to taste

Clean mussels scrape off the threads on the shells.
Rinse under cold running water.
If any are open discard them.
Melt butter in a large saucepan and cook onions and garlic until soft and transparent.
Tip in the mussels, wine and cover.
Cook for 3-4 minutes, or until the shells have all opened.
Discard any mussels that haven't opened.
Pour in the cream and stir well.
Add the coriander, season and serve.

oriental salmon steaks

2 tbsp Hoisin sauce
2 tbsp soy sauce
1tsp sesame oil
A large pinch of five spice powder
1 tbsp clear honey
1 clove garlic, chopped
1 tsp fresh ginger, grated
4 salmon steaks

Combine all the ingredients and add the salmon steaks.
Leave to marinate for at least 2 hours.
Remove the fish from the marinade.
Place under preheated grill or a pan and cook for 6-8 minutes, turning occasionally and basting with the marinade until cooked.

quick baked Asian fish

4 fish fillets
60 ml light soy sauce
2 cm ginger, finely shredded
60 ml sweet chilli sauce
4 spring onions, thinly sliced

Preheat oven to 180 degrees C.
Place fish in a shallow baking dish.
Combine soy sauce, ginger and sweet chilli sauce.
Pour over fish.
Cover with foil and bake for 8 minutes, or until just cooked through.
Serve fish garnished with spring onion.

salmon fillet with a horseradish crust

1 egg yolk
2 tbsp creamed horseradish
50g fresh breadcrumbs
1 tbsp flat leaf parsley, chopped
4 salmon fillets
1 tbsp olive oil
Salt to taste
Freshly ground pepper

Preheat oven to 180 degrees C.
Mix the egg yolk with the horseradish.
Place the breadcrumbs in another dish.
Add the chopped parsley.
Add a little salt and pepper.
Brush the top of the salmon with the horseradish mixture and coat with breadcrumbs.
Heat the oil in a pan until hot.
Place the salmon crust side down.
Cook until the breadcrumbs are beginning to crisp about 3 minutes..
Turn the salmon over and transfer to a baking tray.
Place in the preheated oven for 5 minutes.

steamed fish with garlic and ginger

450g whole fish such as red snapper,
sole or turbot, cleaned and gutted
1 tsp sea salt
½ tsp finely shredded ginger

for the topping

3 tbsp finely shredded spring onion
1 tbsp light soy sauce
2 tsp dark soy sauce
1 tbsp groundnut oil
2 tsp sesame oil
2 cloves garlic, thinly sliced

Remove the gills from the fish wash and pat dry with kitchen paper.
Rub salt on both sides.
Let it rest for 30 minutes.
Put a steamer over a deep pan filled with 5cm of water.
Bring the water to the boil.
Put the fish on a heat proof plate and scatter the ginger evenly over the top.
Put the plate of fish into the steamer.
Cover the pan tightly and gently steam the fish until it is just cooked.
Allow 5 minutes for flat fish, 12 to 14 minutes for whole fish or thicker fish.
Remove the plate of cooked fish.
Sprinkle the spring onions and light and dark soy sauces on top.
Heat the groundnut oil and sesame oil together in a small pan.
When hot, add the garlic slices and brown them.
Pour the garlic oil mixture over the fish.
Serve at once.

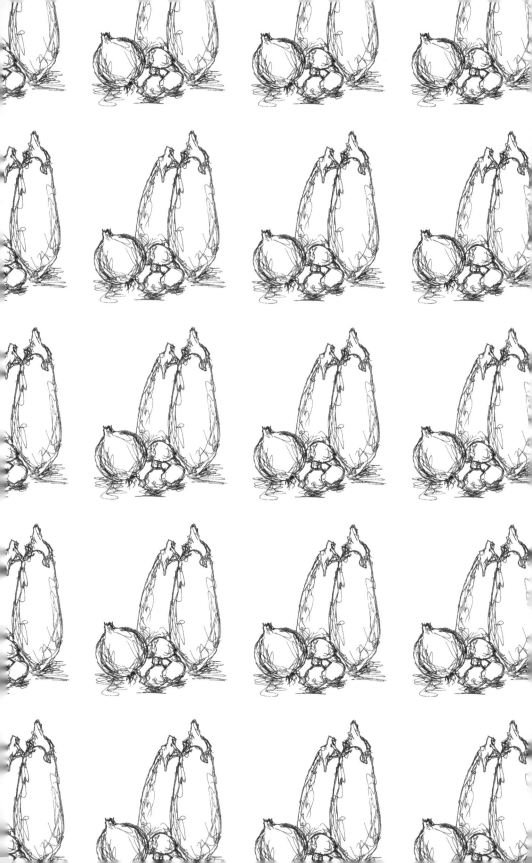

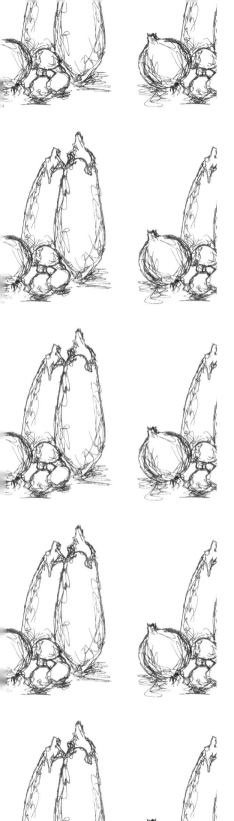

vegetarian

....

beetroot and caramelised onion tart
black bean and tortilla pie
cheese soufflé
masala cheese french toast
middle eastern chickpea stew
paneer spinach pie
pea, paneer and mint frittata
spanish tortilla
spicy vegetable pie
vegetable shepherd's pie
vegetables au gratin
vegetable dumplings

beetroot and caramelised onion tart

175g wholemeal flour
100g porridge oats
100g butter
100g grated carrots
3 large onions, sliced
3 medium beetroots, peeled and grated
3 medium eggs
250 ml milk
Salt to taste
Freshly ground pepper
1½ tbsp oil

Preheat oven to 180 degrees C.
Blitz the butter, oats and flour in a food processor until it resembles breadcrumbs.
Add the grated carrots and blend until the mixture forms a ball.
Roll out and line a 25cm pizza dish or shallow tart case.
Chill.
Heat a little oil in the pan and gently cook the onions for about 15-20 minutes until it begins to caramelise.
Arrange the grated beetroot in the pastry case.
Cover with the caramelised onions.
Whisk the eggs and milk together.
Add salt and pepper to taste.
Pour the whisked egg and milk over the onions and beetroot.
Bake in the oven for 15 minutes.
Lower the temperature to 140 degrees C.
Cook for another 40 minutes until it is firm to touch and golden.

black bean and tortillia pie

3 flour tortilla
2 tsp oil
1 onion, diced
1 jalapeno chilli, deseeded and minced
2 garlic cloves, minced
Salt to taste
Freshly ground pepper
1½ cups water or beer
4 Spring onions, thinly sliced
200g cheddar cheese
2 cans black beans, drained and rinsed
½ tsp cumin, ground
250g sweet corn

Preheat oven to 180 degrees C.
Cut the tortilla to fit a 22cm springform pan.
In a large frying pan heat the oil.
Add the onion, jalapeno, garlic and cumin.
Add a little salt and pepper.
Cook until softened.
Add the beans and water or beer and bring to a boil.
Reduce heat and simmer until all the liquid has evaporated.
Stir in the sweet corn and spring onions and remove from heat.
Place a tortilla in the bottom of the springform pan.
Layer it with quarter of the beans mixture and half a cup of cheese.
Place another layer of tortilla and layer the mixture of beans and cheese.
Repeat.
End with a layer of cheese.
Bake for 20-25 minutes or until the cheese melts.
Remove pie from pan.
Garnish with chopped spring onions.

cheese soufflé

50g unsalted butter
50g plain flour
225 ml milk
5 eggs, separated
140g grated cheddar cheese
Salt to taste
Freshly ground black pepper
¼ tsp cayenne pepper
Pinch mustard powder

Preheat oven to 180 degrees C.
Melt the butter and mix in the flour.
Add the milk and stir until smooth.
Remove from heat when mixture has thickened.
Add the egg yolks, one at a time.
Add the cheese, salt, spices, freshly ground pepper, cayenne pepper and mustard.
Whisk the egg whites until they stand in peaks.
Stir a little egg white into the cheese mixture to loosen it, and then fold in the rest.
Turn the mixture into a buttered soufflé dish.
Bake for 25 minutes until the soufflé is brown and risen.

masala cheese toast

4 slices bread (wholemeal)
4 tsp grated mozzarella cheese
2 tsp oil
2 tbsp finely chopped onions
¼ cup mashed potato
½ tsp finely chopped green chilli
½ tsp chilli powder
¼ tsp garam masala
Salt to taste
2 tbsp fresh coriander, chopped
½ cup finely chopped vegetables (cauliflower, peas, French beans, peppers)

Heat the oil in a pan.
Add the onions and sauté for 30 seconds or till the onions turn translucent.
Add the mixed vegetables, potatoes, green chillies, chilli powder, garam masala,
coriander and salt.
Mix well and cook on a medium flame for 1 to 2 minutes.
Divide the topping into 4 equal portions and keep aside.
Toast the bread slices slightly.
Place the toasted bread slices on a grill tray.
Place the topping on the bread.
Sprinkle each slice with one teaspoon of Mozzarella cheese.
Grill until the cheese melts.
Serve immediately.

middle eastern chick pea stew

900g aubergine
2 large onions
2 cloves garlic, crushed
454g chopped tomatoes
440g can chickpeas, drained
Salt and pepper to taste
1 tbsp oil

Wash and cut the aubergine into slices.
Sprinkle with salt and leave on a paper towel for 30 minutes.
Drain the excess liquid from the aubergine and pat dry.
Preheat oven to 180 degrees C.
Heat the oil in a pan and soften the onions, add the aubergine and garlic.
Mix in the chickpeas and tomatoes and season to taste.
Place the mixture in an ovenproof dish and cover with a lid.
Bake for 40 – 60 minutes.
Serve with pita bread.

Add dried apricots or raisins and cayenne pepper. This gives the stew a
sweet/hot taste.

paneer spinach pie

dough

300g flour
Salt to taste
50g ghee or butter
Cold water as required

Mix flour, salt and ghee to until it resemble breadcrumbs.
Add enough cold water and mix to form dough.
Cover and keep in refrigerator for 20 minutes.

for the paneer

500g paneer, cubed
½ tsp butter
2 onions, chopped fine
1tsp green chilli paste
1tsp garlic paste
1 tbsp tomato sauce
Salt to taste
½ cup cashew nuts, roasted
and powdered

Preheat oven to 180 degrees C.
Heat the butter in a pan
Fry the paneer cubes lightly.
Remove and keep aside.
Add the onions and fry for 2 minutes.
Add the green chilli and garlic paste.
Fry well.
Add the remaining ingredients.
Lastly the paneer cubes.

spinach

½ bunch spinach, chopped fine and cooked
2 onions, grated
2 tsp chilli sauce
2 tsp tomato sauce
½ tsp vinegar
Salt to taste
1 tsp sugar

Drain the spinach and grind coarsely.
Add the remaining ingredients and mix well.
Take half the dough, roll out into a circle.
Line a pie dish.
Trim the edges.
Spread spinach mixture in the pastry case.
Top with the paneer mixture.
Roll out remaining pastry and cover the pie.
Seal edges well.
Brush pie with a little butter.
Bake for 10-15 minutes until done.
Serve hot.

pea, paneer and mint frittata

100g frozen green peas, defrosted
1-2 tbsp olive oil
6 spring onions, finely chopped
100g paneer, crumbled
6 Eggs, lightly whisked
Mint leaves, shredded
Salt to taste
Freshly ground pepper

Heat the grill.
Heat the olive oil in a non-stick frying pan and cook the onions until softened.
Add the lightly whisked eggs, salt, paneer, green peas and mint leaves.
Add pepper and salt to taste.
Stir to combine.
Leave over the heat until the bottom has set.
Slide the pan under the grill to finish off.
Cut the frittata into wedges and serve hot.

spanish tortilla

1kg waxy potatoes, thinly sliced
4 tbsp oil
1 onion, sliced
2 cloves garlic, crushed
1 green pepper, deseeded and sliced
6 large eggs, beaten
2 tomatoes, deseeded and chopped
25g sweet corn
2 tbsp parsley, chopped
Pepper and salt to taste

Parboil the potatoes with a little salt for 5 minutes.
Heat the oil in a large frying pan.
Add the potatoes and onion sauté over low heat.
Stir constantly until the potatoes are browned.
Add the garlic, sweet corn, tomatoes and the green pepper.
Mix well.
Pour the beaten eggs and the parsley and season to taste.
Cook for 12-15 minutes until the underside is cooked.
Preheat grill.
Remove the frying pan from the heat.
Place it under grill for 5-6 minutes or until the tortilla is set and the top is golden.
Serve hot or cold.

spicy vegetable pie

1 tsp coriander powder
1 tsp cumin powder
¼ tsp chilli flakes
½ tsp garam masala
60 ml olive oil
1 large parsnip, cubed
1 onion
2 courgettes, cubed
2 cloves garlic
1 sweet potato, cubed
6 curry leaves, chopped
120g cherry tomatoes, halved
½ tsp paprika
1 egg, lightly beaten
4 shortcrust pastry sheets (25 x 25 cm)

Preheat oven to 200 degrees C.
Mix the coriander powder, cumin powder and garam masala with the oil.
Add the chopped vegetables, garlic, curry leaves.
Season with pepper and salt.
Spread the vegetable mix on a baking tray and bake for 30 minutes.
Add the tomatoes and cook for another 10 minutes.
Cut four 23 cm rounds from the sheets of pastry.
Divide the vegetables into four.
Place the vegetables in the centre of each circle, leaving a border of 3 cm.
Turn in the border, fluting the edges.
Brush pastry with the lightly beaten egg.
Sprinkle with paprika.
Bake for 25 minutes until the pastry is golden.
Serve with mango chutney and raita.

vegetable shepherds pie

1 tbsp olive oil
1 large onion, sliced
500g carrots, cubed
2 tbsp thyme, chopped
200 ml red wine
454g chopped tomatoes
2 vegetable stock cubes
400g cooked lentils
25g butter
85g mature cheddar, grated
150 ml water
950g sweet potato, peeled and cut into chunks

Preheat oven to 170 degrees C.
Heat the oil in a frying pan and fry the onion until golden.
Add the carrots and a sprinkling of thyme.
Pour in the wine and the water.
Add the tomatoes.
Sprinkle in the stock cubes and simmer for 10 minutes.
Add the cooked lentils cover and simmer for another 10 minutes until the carrots still have a bit of bite.
Boil the sweet potato for 15 minutes until tender, drain well.
Mash with the butter.
Add salt and pepper to taste.
Pile the lentil mixture into a pie dish.
Spoon the mash on top.
Sprinkle the cheese and remaining thyme.
Cook for 20 minutes until golden brown.

This pie can be made in advance and chilled for 2 days. If cooking from

chilled bake for 30 minutes.

vegetable au gratin

Assorted vegetables cut into large chunks
1 tbsp butter
1/8 tsp asafoetida powder
1/8 tsp nutmeg
2 tbsp flour
500 ml milk
Freshly ground black pepper
Salt to taste
125g grated cheddar cheese
2 tbsp chopped parsley

Preheat oven to 180 degrees C.
Lightly steam the vegetables.
Melt the butter in a pan.
Remove pan from heat and add the asafoetida and nutmeg.
Stir in the flour and make a smooth paste.
Gradually add the milk, stirring constantly.
Return the pan to the heat and bring the sauce to a boil.
Lower heat and simmer stirring constantly until the sauce is thick and smooth.
Add the salt and pepper to taste and half of the cheese.
Add the steamed vegetables and mix well.
Spoon the mixture into a buttered dish.
Cover with the rest of the grated cheese.
Bake until the top is golden brown about 25 minutes.
Garnish with chopped parsley

The vegetables that could be used - cauliflower, beans, carrots, asparagus, leeks, mushrooms, broccoli, squash, baby potatoes, green peas.

vegetable dumplings

¼ carrot, finely chopped
3 mushrooms, finely chopped
2 water chestnuts, finely chopped
2 bamboo shoots, finely chopped
½ tsp garlic, finely chopped
¼ tsp finely, chopped ginger
10 ml oil
½ tsp sugar
½ tsp sesame oil
Won ton skins
Salt
A little cornstarch

Place a little of the mixture on the centre of the won ton skin.
Wet the sides with a little water.
Gather the corners and make them into little parcels like a draw string purse.
Steam a few dumplings at a time in a steamer.

Meat variation (see pork vegetarian dumplings)

noodles

char kway teow
chicken chow mein
Malaysian stir fried noodles
mee goreng
pad thai noodles
Singapore noodles
Sri Lankan style noodles
vegetarian hakka noodles

char kway teow

....

250g flat rice noodles (kway teow)
100g fresh prawns, shelled
100g cockles, steamed and shelled
100g bean sprouts
100g skinless chicken breast, cut into strips
100g Chinese chives, chopped
½ tbsp light soy sauce
1 tbsp dark soy sauce
1-2 fresh red chillies, finely chopped
3 cloves garlic, finely chopped
2 eggs, beaten
Salt and pepper
1½ tbsp oil

Heat oil in wok and fry the chillies and garlic until fragrant.
Add chicken and stir fry for 2 minutes.
Add prawns and stir fry for another 2 minutes.
Add the cockles.
Add the beaten eggs, stir quickly so that it doesn't become hard or scrambled.
Add the light soy sauce, dark soy sauce and bean sprouts.
Add the noodles and mix thoroughly.
Taste and add salt and pepper to taste.
Stir fry for another 3 minutes and add the chives before turning off the heat.

Kway teow is a kind of white noodles, flat like tagiatelle. Char kway teow means

"stir-fried rice cake strips", is a popular noodle dish in Brunei, Indonesia, Malaysia and

Singapore.

chicken chow mein

150g medium egg noodles
1 tbsp sesame oil
300g chicken breasts, sliced
1 tbsp dark soy sauce
1 tbsp five-spice powder
1 tsp chilli sauce
1 tbsp corn starch
2 tbsp peanut oil
1 red pepper, finely sliced
150g bean sprouts
1 spring onion, sliced lengthways
2 tbsp light soy sauce
Freshly ground black pepper
Dash of sesame oil

Cook the noodles in boiling water until al dente.
Drain, rinse under cold water and drain again.
Drizzle with a little sesame oil and toss.
Place chicken pieces in a bowl.
Add the dark soy sauce, five-spice powder and chilli sauce.
Mix well.
Dust the chicken pieces with corn starch.
Heat the oil in a wok and when hot, add chicken and cook, stirring, until golden brown and cooked through.
Add red pepper, stir fry for a minute.
Add spring onions and bean sprouts, cooking for a further 30 seconds.
Stir in the noodles and season with light soy sauce, a dash of sesame oil and black pepper, to taste.

malaysian stir fried noodles

200g tofu, drained
250g fresh egg noodles
1 tbsp sesame oil
2 garlic cloves, minced
Salt to taste
½ tbsp sugar
1-1½ tbsp chilli paste
1 tbsp fresh lime juice
1 tbsp sweet bean sauce
1 tbsp dark soy sauce
2 tbsp light soy sauce
2 tbsp oil
2 heads baby pak choy trimmed and cut

Line a plate with a triple layer of paper towels.
Put the tofu on top, place a triple layer of paper towels on top of the tofu.
Place another plate on top.
Let stand 20 minutes.
This drains out the liquid from the tofu.
Cut tofu into cubes.
In a large pan of boiling water cook the noodles for 3 minutes or until done.
Drain in a colander over a bowl and, reserve ½ cup of the liquid.
Heat the 2 tablespoons of oil in pan.
Add garlic to pan and cook 30 seconds, stirring constantly.
Add salt and pak choy cook 30 seconds, stirring frequently.
Stir in ¼ cup reserved cooking liquid and bring to a boil.
Reduce heat, and cook for 4 minutes.
Mix the sugar and remaining ingredients, stir until combined.
Add noodles and the remaining ¼ cup cooking liquid to the pan toss to combine.
Cook 30 seconds or until thoroughly heated, tossing to coat.
Add tofu toss to combine.
Serve immediately.

mee goreng

250g yellow noodles
100g fresh green vegetables or cabbage
1 cup bean sprouts
½ fish cake, sliced thinly
100g medium fresh prawns
½ squid, cleaned and cut into pieces
½ tomato, cubed
½-1 onion, sliced
1 tbsp tomato sauce
1 tbsp oyster sauce
½ tsp soy sauce
½ tbsp sugar
Few drops sesame oil
2-3 tbsp chicken stock

blend together

5 dried chilli (soaked in hot water and deseeded)
5 cloves garlic

garnish

Chinese chives (cut into pieces) or coriander leaves

Heat oil in a wok and cook the sliced onions until softened.
Add blended ingredients, cook till fragrant.
Add the oyster sauce, tomato sauce, diced tomato and 2 tablespoons of stock.
Stir and mix well.
Simmer for 1-2 minutes.
Add the prawns, squid and vegetables.
Stir.
Add in sliced fishcake.
Add sugar and the soy sauce.
Stir and mix well.
Add in yellow noodles and bean sprouts.
Mix and cook until the noodles soften and blended well with all the ingredients.
Add 2-3 more tbsp of stock if mee goreng is dry.
Garnish with lime, Chinese chives or coriander leaves.

Mee goreng is a dish of fried noodles. It incorporates a mix of Chinese, Indian, European and Malay flavours.

pad thai noodles

250g dried rice noodles
1-2 eggs or ½ cup soft tofu
4 Spring onions
4 cloves garlic, minced
1 tsp grated galangal or ginger
1 fresh red or green chilli, sliced
3-4 pak choy or Chinese cabbage
2-3 cups bean sprouts
1/3 cup fresh coriander
3-4 tbsp oil for stir-frying
¼ cup chopped unsalted dry roasted peanuts
Lime wedges

sauce

¾ -1½ tbsp tamarind paste
¼ cup vegetable stock
3 ½ tbsp soy sauce
½ -1 tsp chilli sauce
3 tbsp brown sugar
1/8 tsp ground white pepper

Bring a pot of water to a boil and switch off heat.
Soak noodles in the hot water for 4-6 minutes, or until limp but still firm to eat.
Drain and rinse with cold water.
Combine the sauce ingredients in a cup, stirring well until the sugar dissolves.
The sauce should have a sour, sweet, salty and spicy taste.
Set aside.
Warm a wok on medium to high heat.
Add 1-2 tablespoons oil plus the white parts of the spring onions, garlic, galangal or ginger and chilli.
Stir fry for 1 minute to release the fragrance.
Add the pak choy and the stock.
Stir fry for 2 minutes until pak choy is slightly softened.
Push ingredients aside and add half a tablespoon more oil to the wok.
Add the beaten egg and stir fry briefly to scramble.
Add the drained noodles and 1/3 of the sauce.
Stir fry everything together for 1-2 minutes and toss gently.
Keep adding sauce and continue stirring for another 3-6 more minutes, until the noodles are soft but chewy and a little sticky.
Switch off heat and add the bean sprouts and toss them into the hot noodles.
To serve, sprinkle with reserved green onion, fresh coriander, and peanuts.
Add wedges of fresh cut lime on the side.

Substitute – Chilli sauce with cayenne pepper // Peanuts with cashew nuts

White pepper with black pepper

Any leftover sauce can be stored in the refrigerator for up to 3 weeks.

variation: chicken or prawn pad thai – add 150g – 200g chopped chicken breast

or thigh or shelled prawns. Marinade for Chicken/ prawns: 1 tsp. cornstarch dissolved in

3 tbsp soy sauce.

Singapore noodles

125g rice noodles
2 tbsp oil
¼ cup spring onions, sliced
2 cloves garlic, chopped
1 tbsp grated ginger
Handful of green beans
½ red and green pepper, sliced
2½ tsp curry powder
3 tsp soy sauce
6 water chestnuts, sliced
A few slices of lotus root
¼ tsp turmeric powder
2 tsp rice wine
¼ tsp sugar
5 Shitake mushrooms slices
50g prawns
50g char sui pork or chicken, shredded
1 green chilli finely chopped
1 egg, beaten with a pinch of salt and a splash of sesame oil

garnish
Spring onion greens chopped

Soak noodles in hot water until soft.
Drain.
Blanch the green beans and set aside.
Into the noodles add half the curry powder and all the soy sauce, wine and sugar.
Toss together the noodles until well coated.
Heat oil in a wok and fry the garlic and ginger for 30 seconds.
Tip in the vegetables.
Stir fry for a couple of minutes.
Then push the vegetables to the side of the wok and tip in the egg.
Allow to cook undisturbed until almost set, then scramble into the remaining ingredients.
Add the noodles and the rest of the ingredients and mix well.
Serve hot garnished with spring onion greens.

Sri Lankan style noodles

300g rice noodles, boiled
Strain and rinse through with cold water

225g cabbage, thinly sliced
225g leeks, thinly sliced
225g carrots, thinly sliced
225g beans, thinly sliced
1 tbsp chopped garlic
1 tsp chopped ginger
4 - 6 green chillies (optional)
½ tsp pepper powder
1½ tsp salt
1 tbsp soy sauce
1 tbsp tomato sauce
½ onion chopped
3 tbsp vegetable oil

Heat the oil in a wok and add the chopped onions, the green chillies, garlic and ginger.
When the onions are slightly golden in colour add the vegetables, pepper and salt.
Stir and cook for about 5 minutes.
The vegetables should be crisp.
Take off fire and add the sauces.
Toss in the noodles and mix well.
Warm the vegetables and noodles.
Serve with chicken, lamb or soya meat curry.

vegetarian hakka noodles

200g hakka noodles
4 medium spring onions finely chopped
1 small carrot grated
10 French beans, finely sliced
5 button mushrooms finely chopped
1 medium bell pepper, finely sliced
3 red or green chillies, deseeded and sliced
1 tsp finely chopped fresh coriander
1 piece of ginger finely chopped
½ tsp rice wine
2 tbsp oil
2 tsp soy sauce
Salt and pepper to taste

Boil the noodles in a pan of water.
Drain and rinse the noodles in cold running water.
Add the oil to the noodles and mix well. Keep aside.
In a wok heat the oil.
Sauté the garlic, ginger and chillies.
Add the finely chopped spring onions and French beans.
Cook for 3 minutes.
Add the mushrooms, carrot, pepper and coriander.
Season with salt and pepper and add the rice wine.
Stir fry the vegetables for 5 – 6 minutes.
Add the soy sauce.
Toss the noodles into the wok and cook on high heat for 1 minute.
Garnish with chopped spring onions and serve.

Hakka noodles are made with rice or wheat flour.

stuffed /wraps

chapatti wrap
quesadillas
stuffed mushrooms
stuffed peppers

chapati ⌒wrap

4 chapatis
250g cooked chicken or lamb
Rocket leaves
Tomato, cubed
Cucumber, cubed
Onions, cubed
Mint leaves, chopped
Yogurt

Shred the chicken or lamb into small pieces.
In a bowl mix together a little yogurt and the mint leaves.
Toss the meat in the yogurt mixture.
Heat a chapati.
Place a little rocket leaves in the middle.
Then the chicken yogurt mixture.
Fold the bottom end of the chapati.
The roll the sides to make the wrap.

variation
Use light mayonnaise mixed with a little curry powder.
Yogurt with a little tahini paste.

quesadillas

Spring onions, chopped
Fresh coriander, chopped
Green chilli, deseeded and chopped
Grated cheese
Tortillas

Mix the spring onions, coriander, green chilli and cheese.
Sprinkle on a tortilla, cover with another and press down.
Heat a non stick frying pan.
Place the tortilla to cook for about a minute.
Turn it over and cook the other side.
Cut into quarters and serve with guacamole.
You can also use finely sliced chicken or tomato.

stuffed mushrooms

1 small onion, chopped
2 large open mushrooms per person
25g smoked rind less bacon, chopped
A little butter
50g soft cream cheese
25g breadcrumbs
Fresh parsley chopped
A little grated cheese
50g butter
Salt and pepper to taste

Pre-heat oven to 180 degrees C.
Chop the stalks off the mushrooms.
Melt the butter, add the mushroom stalks, bacon and onion and cook for 8-10 minutes.
In a bowl mix the cooked ingredients with the cream cheese.
Add half the breadcrumbs.
Place the filling into the mushrooms.
Mix the parsley, the rest of the breadcrumbs and the grated cheese and sprinkle over the mushroom.
Place the mushrooms in a buttered dish.
Bake for 20 minutes.

stuffed peppers

4 Peppers
2 tbsp oil
Bunch of spring onions, sliced
½ tsp chilli powder
200g chicken, beef, lamb or pork mince
½ tsp paprika
½ tsp ground cumin
½ tsp ground coriander
227g can chopped tomatoes
100g carrot, grated
50g sultanas (optional)
250g couscous or rice, cooked
100 ml chicken stock
2 tbsp flat leaf parsley, chopped

Preheat oven to 170 degrees C.
Place the peppers in a cup cake or muffin tray.
Cut the tops off the peppers.
Scoop out the pith and seeds.
Heat the oil in a pan and fry the spring onions.
Transfer to a bowl.
Add the mince to the pan and cook until browned.
Add the spices, tomatoes, carrot, sultanas and stock.
Cover and simmer for 10 minutes.
Add the cooked rice or the couscous.
Fill the peppers with the mixture and replace the tops and bake for 15 minutes.
Serve the stuffed peppers garnished with chopped parsley.

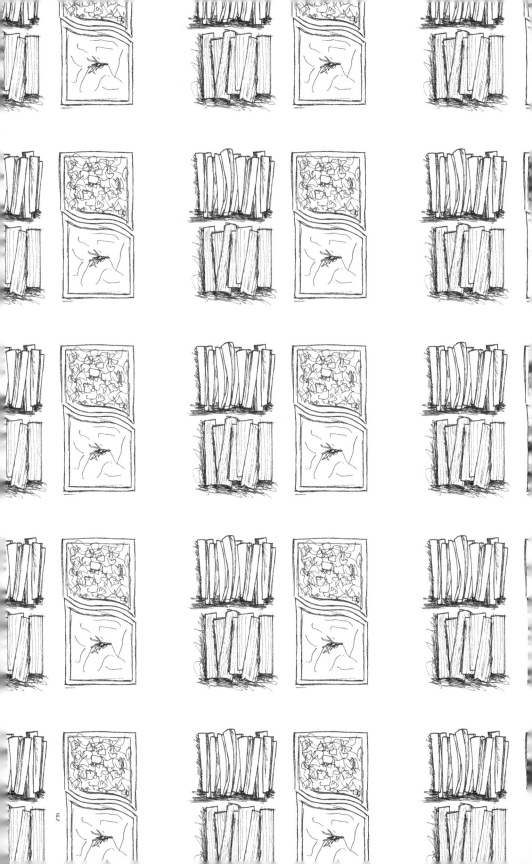

dips

·····················

almond hummus
baba ganoush
cheese, thyme and garlic dip
clam or crabmeat dip
curry dip
guacamole
hummus
mango salsa
onion dip
salsa

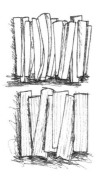

almond hummus

2 cups soaked almonds
½ cup tahini
1 clove garlic finely chopped
Juice of 2 large lemons
¼-½ tsp sea salt
1 tbsp freshly chopped parsley
1 tsp basil, chopped

In a food processor or blender blitz the almonds.
Add the other ingredients and mix well to a smooth consistency.
Add a little water if necessary.
Make it chunky to spread on crackers or smooth for a dip.

Chunky and smooth, they taste different.

baba ganoush

....

1 large aubergine
4 cloves garlic, chopped
2 tbsp tahini
Juice of 1 lemon
½ cup fresh parsley, chopped
Pinch of cumin powder
¼ cup olive oil

Preheat oven to 230 degrees C.
Slice aubergine in half, prick with a fork.
Bake until the flesh is soft about 25-30 minutes.
Mix the aubergine, garlic, tahini, lemon juice and parsley in a food processor.
Toss in the cumin and slowly add the olive oil and blend everything together.

cheese, thyme and garlic dip

1 tbsp fresh thyme
1 clove garlic
½ tsp sea salt
¼ tsp ground black pepper
200g cream cheese
¼ cup sour cream

Blend the thyme, garlic, salt and pepper in a food processor until garlic is finely chopped.
Add the cheese and sour cream and mix.
Transfer dip into a bowl and chill for 30 minutes before serving.

This dip can be made up to a day in advance.

clam or crabmeat dip

250g cream cheese
1 can clams or crabmeat, minced
Dash of Worcestershire sauce
Sea salt to taste

Soften cream cheese with a small amount of juice from the clam or crabmeat.
Add the rest of the ingredients.
Refrigerate at least 2 hours best left overnight.

curry dip

1½ cups mayonnaise
½ tsp curry powder
2 cloves garlic chopped finely
A drop of Tabasco sauce
Lemon juice
1 tbsp chopped parsley
Salt and pepper

Mix well together.
Chill before serving with vegetable sticks.

guacamole

....

2 Avocados, peeled and quartered
4 tbsp sour cream
2 tbsp mayonnaise
2 tbsp lemon juice
1 clove garlic
1 tbsp chopped onions
2- 4 green chillies deseeded and chopped
Salt and pepper to taste

Combine all ingredients in a blender and blend until smooth.
Transfer the mixture into a bowl.
Cover with a wax paper against surface to prevent discolouration.
Chill until ready to serve.
Serve with corn chips or pita bread toasted until crispy.

hummus

450g can of chickpeas
¼ cup liquid from can of chickpeas
3-5 tbsp lemon juice
1½ tbsp tahini
2 cloves garlic, crushed
½ tsp salt
2 tbsp olive oil
Chopped parsley

Drain chickpeas and set aside the liquid from can.
Combine remaining ingredients in blender or food processor.
Add quarter cup of liquid from the chickpeas.
Blend for 3-5 minutes until thoroughly mixed and smooth.
Place in serving bowl, and create a shallow well in the centre of the hummus.
Add 1-2 tablespoons of olive oil in the well.
Garnish with parsley.

mango salsa

1 Mango, peeled and cubed
2 tbsp chopped coriander leaves
1 shallot, finely chopped
Juice of 1 lime
Freshly ground salt and pepper
2 tbsp olive oil
1 red chilli, deseeded and finely chopped

Mix the ingredients together and season with salt.
Chill until ready to serve.

onion dip

8 tsp dried onion flakes or 1 packet onion soup mix
1½ tsp dried parsley
1 tsp onion powder
1 tsp turmeric
½ tsp celery seeds
Salt to taste
½ tsp sugar
Freshly ground black pepper
½ tsp garlic powder

Mix ingredients well with sour cream.
Chill well before serving.

salsa
....

6 large ripe tomatoes, peeled, deseeded and diced
1 large onion, chopped
1 red pepper, deseeded, and chopped
2 cloves garlic, minced
2 tbsp red wine vinegar
1 tbsp olive oil
½ tsp dried oregano
3 tbsp coriander leaves chopped
2 Jalapeno peppers, seeded and minced

Combine all ingredients.
Toss well.
Refrigerate at least for 4 hours.

May be made 3 days in advance.

desserts

black forest trifle
caramel trifle
chocolate biscuit gateau
chocolate mousse
coffee mousse
jelly snow
lime cheesecake
peach cobbler
pineapple pudding
pumpkin cheesecake bars
strawberry mallow mousse
sweet potato pie

black forest trifle

2 chocolate sponge cakes
1 can cherry pie filling
Cherry Jam
Cherries

custard

500 ml milk
2 tbsp custard powder
2 tbsp cocoa powder

Warm the milk.
Mix the custard powder and cocoa powder in a little milk.
Add to the warm milk and cook stirring continuously until it thickens.
Place the cakes at the bottom of a bowl.
Top the cakes with the cherry pie filling, along with the jam.
Pour the custard over.
Let it set in the refrigerator.
Decorate with cherries.

caramel trifle
....

4-8 sponge fingers
125 ml water
Strawberry jam
2 tbsp brandy
200g sugar
500 ml milk
3 eggs

Beat the three eggs well.
Add 500 ml milk and cook on a low flame until it thickens.
Let it cool.
Spread jam on the sponge fingers and place in the bottom of dish.
Soak the sponge fingers with the brandy.
Dissolve sugar in a pan of water, on a low flame continuously stir until sugar caramelises.
Add prepared custard and blend gently over a low flame.
Pour over sponge fingers.
Cool and leave to set in refrigerator.
Decorate with cream and nuts.

chocolate biscuit gateau

··

100g sugar
2 tbsp cocoa
150 ml cream
1 cup milk
Vanilla
100g roasted cashew nuts
3 eggs, separated
200g Marie biscuits (substitute digestives or rich tea biscuits)

Cream the butter and sugar together.
Add the egg yolks one at a time.
Then add the cocoa and the vanilla essence.
Beat the egg whites until stiff and frothy.
Add to the cream.
Toss in some nuts and mix into the cream.
Soak the biscuits in milk.
Arrange a layer of biscuits in a pudding dish.
Pour in a layer of cream mixture, then a layer of biscuits.
End with a layer of cream.
Leave to set.
Sprinkle with nuts before serving.

chocolate mousse

4 egg yolks
6 egg whites
150g unsalted butter
250g chocolate
500ml whipped cream

Melt the chocolate and butter.
Beat the egg yolks and add to the chocolate and butter mixture.
Whisk the egg whites until very stiff and slowly add the sugar beating continuously.
Fold in the chocolate mixture and lastly add the whipped cream.
Pour into a pudding dish.
Leave to set in refrigerator.

coffee mousse

2 eggs, separated
100g castor sugar
3 tbsp instant coffee granules
300 ml double cream

decoration
sponge fingers and chocolate curls

Place the egg yolks and sugar in a bowl over a pan of hot water and whisk until thick and creamy.
Remove from heat and whisk until cool.
Stir in the coffee granules dissolved in a little water.
Whip the cream until soft peaks form.
Add to the coffee mixture, blend well.
Spoon into individual dishes and chill.
Decorate with chocolate swirls and serve with sponge fingers.

jelly snow

1 packet strawberry or raspberry jelly
375 ml of water
200 ml evaporated milk
200 ml hot water
2 tbsp rum
3 eggs
75g sugar
1½ tbsp gelatine
Fruits – mango, pineapple, strawberries or whatever fruits you like

Mix the jelly crystals in hot water until dissolved.
Wet either an oval or rectangular dish.
Pour a very thin layer of jelly and let it set.
Arrange the fruit on top of the thin layer of jelly.
Leave to set again.
Add 1 tablespoon of rum to the rest of the jelly and gently pour over the fruit.
Leave to set.
Beat the yolks of eggs.
Add the evaporated milk, water, sugar and cook on a low heat until it thickens.
Cool the custard.
Dissolve the gelatine in ¼ cup of hot water.
Add the gelatine and a little more rum to the custard.
Beat the white of eggs with a pinch of salt until it is stiff.
Fold the egg whites into custard.
Pour over set jelly and set again.
Turn out on a flat tray and decorate with the balance fruit.

lime cheesecake

400g digestive biscuits
200g butter
500g cream cheese
397g can of condensed milk
4 limes juiced and zest
250 ml whipping cream

Crush the biscuits.
Melt the butter and mix into the crushed biscuits.
Line a loose bottom pan with foil.
Put the biscuit crumbs and press in well.
Mix all the other ingredients together, reserving some zest for decoration.
Pour over the biscuit base and chill in the refrigerator.
Refrigerate until well set.
Remove from pan.
Sprinkle a little lime zest on top and serve.

Lime can be replaced with strawberries, blackberries or passion fruit.

peach cobbler

410g can peaches in light syrup, sliced
1/3 cup brown sugar
¼ cup granulated sugar
Juice of 1 lemon
¼ tsp ground cinnamon
¼ tsp ground nutmeg
A pinch of salt
1 tbsp butter
2 tbsp corn starch
1½ cup sifted flour
1 tsp baking powder
½ tsp salt
2 tsp sugar
1/3 cup butter
1/3 cup milk

Preheat oven to 200 degree C.
Drain peaches, reserve the syrup.
Arrange peach slices in a lightly buttered baking dish.
Measure 1 cup of the syrup into a small saucepan, blend in the sugars, lemon juice, spices, salt, butter, and corn starch.
Place the saucepan over medium heat.
Bring to a boil and simmer, stirring, until it thickens.
Pour the hot mixture over the peaches.
Place in the oven while preparing the topping.
Sift together the flour, baking powder, salt and 2 teaspoons sugar.
Mix in the butter.
The mixture should resemble coarse breadcrumbs.
Add milk and stir until stiff dough is formed.
Drop spoonfuls onto the hot peach filling.
Return to the oven and bake until topping is browned, about 20 minutes.
Serve warm, with vanilla ice cream or whipped cream.

pineapple pudding

397g can of condensed milk
10g gelatine
3 tbsp corn flour
2 tbsp sugar
1 pineapple medium size
Handful of raisins
1 tsp vanilla
1¾ cans water (use the condensed milk can)

Peel and slice the pineapple into small pieces.
Cook the pineapple on a low flame adding 2 tablespoons of sugar.
Cook until the colour changes to a light golden brown.
Remove from fire and let it cool.
Dissolve the gelatine in a small amount of warm water.
Keep aside.
Dissolve corn flour in water.
Keep aside.
Mix condensed milk and water in a pan.
Cook on moderate heat stir continuously until it starts to boil.
Add vanilla, pineapple and raisins reserving some pineapple and raisins for the garnish.
Continue stirring.
Add corn flour and continue stirring.
When the mixture thickens switch off the fire and add the gelatine.
Pour the mixture in to a dish and garnish with the reserved pineapple and raisins.
Refrigerate until it is well set 5-6 six hours.

pumpkin cheesecake bars

pumpkin pie spice

3 tbsp ground cinnamon
2 tsp ground ginger
2 tsp ground nutmeg
1½ tsp ground all spice
1½ tsp ground cloves

Mix all together and store in airtight
container.

450g digestive biscuits, crushed
2 eggs
2 tbsp melted butter
½ tsp salt
4 tsp pumpkin pie spice
250g cream cheese
397g can of condensed milk
450g can pumpkin
1 cup chopped nuts

Preheat oven to 170 degrees C.
In a large bowl, combine the biscuit crumbs, melted butter and 2 teaspoons of the
pumpkin pie spice.
Press onto the bottom of a Swiss roll tin.
Set aside.
Beat the cream cheese in a bowl until fluffy.
Gradually beat in the condensed milk.
Add the remaining eggs, pumpkin, the pumpkin spice and salt.
Mix well.
Pour over crust.
Sprinkle nuts on top.
Bake for 35 minutes or until set.
Cool.
Chill and cut into bars.
Keep in refrigerator.

strawberry mallow mousse

85g strawberry jelly crystals
2 tbsp lemon juice
1 cup water
300 ml cream
1/3 cup milk
200g white marshmallow
Fresh strawberries

Make the jelly and let it set a little.
Combine the marshmallows and milk.
Stir on a gentle heat to melt the marshmallows a little.
Cool.
Beat the cream and add to marshmallow mixture.
Add the chopped berries, lemon juice and jelly.
Stir once and pour into a lightly oiled mould.
Let it set in the refrigerator.
Turn out and serve.

sweet potato pie

450g sweet potato
½ cup butter
1cup sugar
½ cup milk
2 eggs
½ tsp ground nutmeg
½ tsp cinnamon
1 tsp vanilla extract
1 unbaked pie crust (20 cm)

two crust pastry

2 cups flour
1 tsp salt
2/3 cup + 4-5 tbsp cold water

Mix into a dough and line a 20 cm pie dish.

Preheat oven to 170 degrees C.
Boil the sweet potatoes whole with skin for 30 minutes or until done.
Run cold water over the sweet potato and remove skin.
Mash with the butter.
Stir in the sugar, milk, eggs, nutmeg, cinnamon and vanilla extract.
Beat with a whisk until the mixture is smooth.
Pour the filling into an unbaked crust.
Bake for 45-55 minutes or until knife inserted in centre comes out clean.
Pie will puff up like a soufflé and then will sink down as it cools.

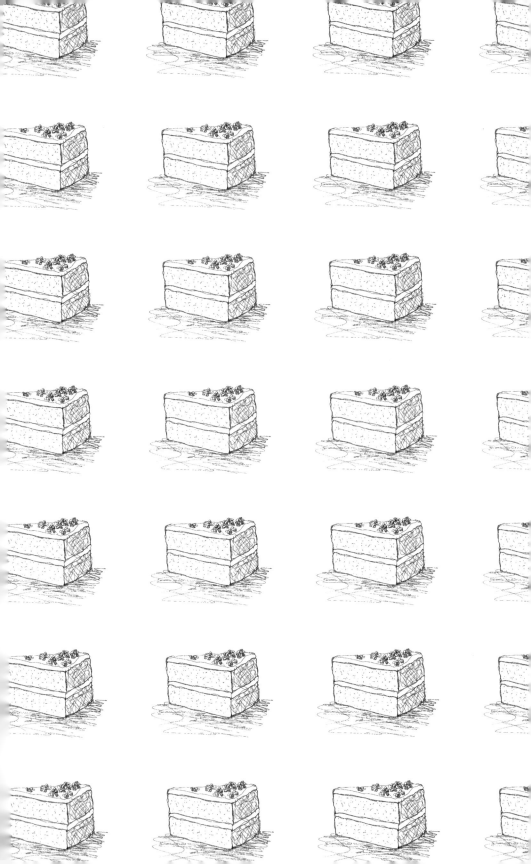

cakes

banana cake
blueberry cake
carrot cake
chocolate beetroot cake
coffee and walnut cake
eggless sponge cake
fruit cake (Sri Lankan)
love cake
pineapple cake
pineapple upside down cake
red velvet cake
simnel cake

banana cake

100g butter or margarine
200g sugar
3 bananas
2 eggs
1 tsp bicarbonate of soda
225g self raising flour
2 tbsp milk

Preheat oven to 170 degrees C.
Cream the butter and sugar.
Add the eggs one at a time and beat well.
Add the mashed bananas, flour mixed with the bicarbonate of soda and milk.
Pour into a greased lined tin.
Bake for 30-35 minutes.
Stick a tooth pick in the centre of the cake and if it comes out clean the cake is done.

blueberry cake

1½ cups sugar
125g butter
100g cream cheese
3 eggs
1 egg white
3 cups plain flour
2 cups fresh or frozen blueberries
1 tsp baking powder
½ tsp bicarbonate of soda
½ tsp salt
200g vanilla or lemon yogurt
2 tsp vanilla

glaze
½ cup icing sugar
4 tsp fresh lemon juice

Preheat the oven to 170 degrees C.
In a mixing bowl, cream together the butter and sugar.
Add the three eggs and the egg white and beat well.
Remove 2 tablespoons of flour and mix with blueberries.
Add flour, baking powder, bicarbonate of soda and salt alternately to the butter mixture.
Add vanilla and carefully fold in the blueberries, yogurt and cream cheese.
Pour into a greased floured cake tin.
Bake for 40 - 50 minutes until the cake is cooked through.
Cool in tin for 15 minutes before removing to a cooling rack.
Dust with icing sugar.

carrot cake

2½ cup grated carrot
1 cup oil
3 eggs
1 cup castor sugar
1 cup orange juice
½ tsp nutmeg powder
1 tsp cardamom powder
2 cups flour, sifted
½ tsp salt
1 cup chopped walnuts

frosting

1 cup cream cheese
2 tsp orange juice
2 tbsp honey

Whisk together and leave in freezer
for at least 30 minutes.

Preheat oven to 170 degrees C.
Line and grease a cake tin.
Squeeze the grated carrot to remove excess water.
Set aside.
Mix together the oil, eggs, sugar and orange juice in a bowl.
Whisk to a thick batter.
Add the nutmeg, cardamom and salt.
Whisk again.
Add the grated carrot and the ground walnuts.
Transfer to cake pan and bake until done.
Cool the cake.
Cut the cake in half horizontally and layer with a little frosting.
Assemble the two halves and spread frosting over the cake.
Decorate with some walnuts.

chocolate beetroot cake

50g cooked beetroots, pureed
½ tsp vanilla
250g caster sugar
250 ml vegetable oil
3 eggs
225g plain flour
1½ tsp bicarbonate of soda
¼ tsp salt
6 tbsp unsweetened cocoa powder

Preheat oven to 170 degrees C.
Grease and line a 20 x 30cm baking tin.
Combine the pureed beetroots, eggs, vanilla, oil and sugar in a large bowl.
Mix with an electric mixer on low speed until well mixed.
In a separate bowl, mix together flour, bicarbonate of soda, salt and cocoa.
Add to the creamed mixture, beat well.
Pour batter into prepared tin.
Bake for 25 to 30 minutes until done.
Cool.
Cover with icing of your choice.

coffee and walnut cake

....

225g flour
225g castor sugar
225g unsalted butter
150g chopped walnuts
100 ml strong coffee
4 eggs
1 tsp baking powder

Preheat oven to 170 degrees C.
Put all the ingredients except the walnuts and the coffee whisk together until smooth.
Add the walnuts and mix them in so that they are evenly distributed.
Pour in the coffee and mix well.
Pour the mixture into 2 greased lined cake tins, bake for 30 to 35 minutes or until done.

icing

250g unsalted butter
200g icing sugar
4 tbsp strong coffee
Walnuts, to decorate

While the cake is cooling make the butter cream.
Sandwich the cakes with a little butter cream.
Spread the rest of the butter cream on top of the cake and decorate with walnuts.

eggless sponge cake

200g condensed milk
140g self raising flour
1 tsp baking powder
½ tsp bicarbonate of soda
60 ml melted butter or margarine
1 tsp vanilla essence
75ml water

Preheat oven to 170 degrees C.
Grease and line a 15cm diameter tin.
Sieve the flour, baking powder and the bicarbonate of soda together.
Into the flour add the condensed milk, melted butter, vanilla, 75 ml water and beat well.
Pour the mixture into a greased and dusted cake tin.
Bake for 10 minutes.
Then reduce the heat to 140 degrees C.
Bake for a further 10 minutes.
The cake is ready when it leaves the sides of the tin and is springy to touch.
Take out from the oven and leave for 1 minute.
Invert the tin over a rack and tap sharply to remove.
Cool the cake.

fruit cake (Sri Lankan)

450g semolina
25 yolks of eggs
450g sugar
450g sultanas
450 cherries
1 jar ginger in syrup
450g cashew nuts
450g butter
12 egg whites, beaten
300g pumpkin preserve
450 raisins
1 jar chow chow
100g candied peel
1 tbsp rose essence
2 tbsp vanilla essence
1 tbsp honey
1 bottle strawberry jam (optional)
1 tbsp almond essence
1 wine glass brandy
2 teaspoons spice powder (cardamom, cloves, nutmeg, cinnamon ground together)

Chop all the fruits and pour half of the essences and spices, mix well and leave in an air tight jar for 3 days.
Preheat oven to 150 degrees C.
Slightly roast the semolina and when cool, mix with the butter and set aside.
Beat 25 yolks of eggs and sugar together.
Add the fruit mixture and then the semolina and butter.
Add all the balance of spices and essences and the jam.
Lastly add the stiffly beaten whites of eggs and mix well.
Pour into a tray which has been lined with greaseproof paper and bake for about 2 ½ to 3 hours.

Substitute for pumpkin preserve - petha.

Substitute for chow chow – melon and ginger jam.

Found in Asian Supermarkets.

love cake
....

375g raw unsalted cashews
200g unsalted butter
315g caster sugar
8 egg yolks
250g semolina
80ml honey
2 tsp rosewater
1 tsp ground cardamom
1 tsp ground cinnamon
¼ tsp nutmeg
4 egg whites
Icing sugar, to dust

Preheat oven to 150 degrees C.
Grease and line a 20cm square cake tin.
Chops the cashew nuts finely in a food processor.
Set aside.
Whisk the butter and sugar in a large bowl until very pale and creamy.
Add the egg yolks, one at a time, beating well after each addition.
Use a large metal spoon to fold in the cashew nuts, semolina, honey, rosewater, cardamom, cinnamon and nutmeg.
In a separate bowl, whisk the egg whites until firm peaks form.
Fold into semolina mixture.
Spoon the cake mixture into the prepared pan.
Bake in oven for 1 hour 10 minutes or until firm to the touch.
Turn oven off.
Leave the cake in the oven, with the door slightly ajar, to cool completely.
Cut into pieces and dust with icing sugar to serve.

pineapple cake

2 cups of plain flour
2 cups castor sugar
1 tsp bicarbonate of soda
1 cup chopped walnuts
½ tsp salt
¾ cup vegetable oil
450g crushed pineapple with juice

Preheat oven to 170 degrees C.
Mix together the flour, salt, eggs, sugar, bicarbonate of soda and oil.
Stir in the pineapple with the juice and the walnuts.
Pour the batter into a greased, lined cake tin 22 cm x 33 cm.
Bake the cake for 45 minutes or until it is cooked through.
Cool on a wire rack.

icing

250g cream cheese
2 cups icing sugar
½ cup butter
1 tsp vanilla extract

Cream together the cheese, butter and the icing sugar and vanilla.
Cover the cake with the icing.

pineapple upside down cake

300g unsalted butter
250g golden syrup
6 fresh or canned pineapple rings
6 glacé cherries
300g caster sugar
300g self raising flour
4 medium eggs, lightly beaten
6-8 tbsp milk

Preheat the oven to 170 degrees C.
Grease and line a deep 30 x 23cm baking dish.
Pour the golden syrup into the tin, pop in the oven and heat for 2 minutes.
Tilt the tin to evenly spread the syrup.
Top with the pineapple rings, putting a glacé cherry in the middle of each ring.
If you don't like cherries you can leave this out.
In a large bowl, cream the butter and sugar until fluffy.
Gradually beat in the eggs, fold in the flour and enough milk to make smooth consistency.
Spoon the mixture into the dish, making sure that the surface is level.
Bake for 35 to 40 minutes, or until golden.
Leave to cool in the dish for 30 minutes.
Carefully turn the cake out on to a board.
Cut into slices and serve warm or at room temperature.

red velvet cake

2 cups flour
1 tsp bicarbonate of soda
1 tsp baking powder
1 tsp salt
2 tbsp unsweetened cocoa powder
2 cups sugar
1 cup vegetable oil
2 eggs
1 cup buttermilk
2 teaspoon vanilla extract
1-2 tbsp red food colouring
1 tsp white vinegar
½ cup hot strong black coffee

Preheat oven 170 degrees C.
Grease and flour two 22 cm cake tins.
Sieve together the flour, bicarbonate of soda, baking powder, cocoa powder and salt.
Set aside.
In a large bowl, combine the sugar and vegetable oil.
Mix in the eggs, buttermilk, vanilla and red food colouring until combined.
Add the coffee and white vinegar and mix well.
Add the dry ingredients a little at time, mixing just until combined.
Pour the batter evenly into each pan.
Bake in the middle rack for 30 to40 minutes.
To test whether cake is done, stick a toothpick in the centre of the cake and if it comes out clean the cake is done.
Let it cool in the tins for 15 minutes.
Remove the cakes from the tins and let them cool on wire racks.
Sandwich the two cakes with a little frosting.
Cover the cake with cream cheese frosting.

 Substitutes for buttermilk

200ml plain yogurt to 50 ml whole or semi-skimmed milk

If using Greek yogurt; equal quantities of yogurt and whole or semi-skimmed milk.

250 ml whole or semi skimmed milk plus 1 tbsp of lemon juice or white wine

vinegar. Stir well and leave to stand for 5 minutes before using.

simnel cake

225g butter
100g cherries, chopped
200g light muscovado sugar
4 large eggs
225g flour
500g mixed dried fruits
50g candied peel
100g ginger preserve, chopped
2 lemons, grated zest only
A little grated nutmeg
2 tsp ground mixed spice
1 tsp baking powder

filling and topping
450g marzipan
1-2 tbsp apricot jam, warmed

Preheat the oven to 150 degrees C.
Grease and line a 20cm diameter cake tin.
Cut the cherries into quarters.
Mix the cherries, mixed dried fruits, candied peel, ginger preserve lemon zest and mixed spice with the self raising flour.
Whisk the butter and sugar until light and fluffy.
Add the eggs one at a time and continue beating.
Add the flour to the fruit mixture.
Pour half the mixture into the prepared tin.
Take one-third of the marzipan and roll it out into a circle the size of the tin and then place on top of the cake mixture.
Spoon the remaining cake mixture on top and level the surface.
Bake for about 2½ hours, or until well risen, evenly browned and firm to the touch.
Cover with aluminium foil after one hour if the top is browning too quickly.
Leave to cool in the tin for 10 minutes.
Turn out the cake and finish cooling on a wire rack.
Brush the top with a little warmed apricot jam.
Roll out half the remaining marzipan to fit the top.
Press firmly on the top and crimp the edges to decorate.
Form the remaining marzipan into 11 balls.
Arrange the marzipan balls around the edge of the cake.
Brush the tops of the balls with beaten egg and then carefully place the cake under a hot grill until the top is lightly toasted.

icings

butter icing
cream cheese frosting
glace frosting
high humidity icing
royal icing
water icing

butter icing

200g icing sugar
Food colouring
100g butter
Flavouring

Sieve the sugar and the butter a little at a time and beat to a cream.
Add the flavouring and desired colour and mix well.

chocolate icing
Add 50g grated chocolate or cocoa.

coffee icing
Add strong black coffee to taste to the butter icing.

lemon icing
Add lemon juice

When you touch the icing it should not stick to your fingers.

If it does, then add a little more sugar.

cream cheese frosting

125g unsalted butter
250g cream cheese
450g icing sugar

Cream the butter in a bowl until soft.
Add half the icing sugar and mix until combined.
Add half the cream cheese and mix again.
Repeat until all the ingredients are thoroughly combined and frosting is light and creamy.
Leave it in the refrigerator for 30-60 minutes before piping on to the cake.

glace frosting

2 cups icing sugar
2 tbsp soft butter
2 tbsp boiling water

Sift the icing sugar into a bowl.
Add the softened butter and hot water.
Whisk until smooth.
Spread the frosting over the cake.

variations

chocolate
Add 1 tbsp cocoa powder

vanilla
Replace boiling water with milk and add a couple of drops of vanilla essence.

lemon or orange
Replace boiling water with lemon/orange juice.

passionfruit
Replace boiling water with passion fruit pulp and 1 tsp lemon juice.

coffee
Dissolve one teaspoon of instant coffee granules into the boiling water.

mocha
Sift 2 teaspoons of cocoa powder into icing sugar and dissolve one teaspoon of instant coffee granules into the boiling water.

high humidity icing

1 ½ cup margarine or (Crisco)
½ tsp flavouring
1-1 ½ tbsp corn flour
¼ tsp salt
¼ cup milk
500g sifted icing sugar approximately

Mix margarine, milk, flavouring and salt well.
Add the corn flour, and then add sugar gradually.
Do not over mix.
(It is impossible to be exact about the quantity of icing sugar)
A nice firm mixture which holds peaks is required.
If it is too stiff you can always add a little milk to soften the icing.

This icing pipes beautifully and when it dries it is firm to the touch but soft on

the inside. There is no need to store the cake in the refrigerator when first made it will

not melt even if kept out in hot weather.

royal icing

500g icing sugar
½ -1 tbsp lime juice
3 whites of eggs
Colouring

Sieve the sugar into a bowl.
And the egg whites little at a time and whisk.
Add lime juice a few drops at a time.
Whisk until the mixture is light and very white.
This can be used to decorate a cake or make flowers using icing nozzles.

water icing

200g icing sugar
2 tbsp water
Flavouring
Colouring

Sieve the sugar and put into a saucepan.
Add the water a little at a time and stir over a slow fire with a wooden spoon until warm.
Do not allow to boil.
Icing should be thick enough to coat the wooden spoon.
Remove from fire, flavour and colour as desired and pour over the cake.

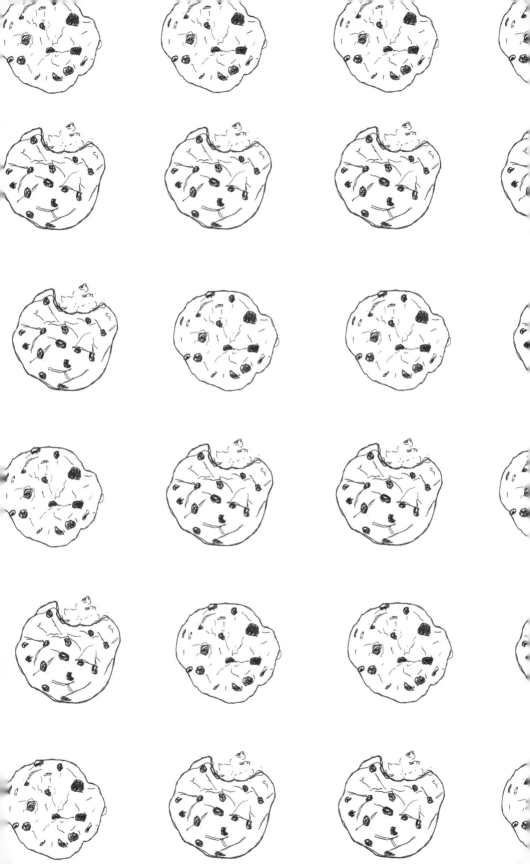

biscuits / cookies

butter biscuits
chocolate chip cookies
cinnamon cookies
eggless chocolate chip cookies
ginger biscuits with stem ginger
melting moments
napolitas
spiced biscuits

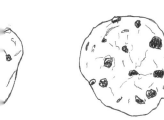

butter biscuits

250g flour
100g butter
1 tsp vanilla
150g sugar
1 egg
1 tsp baking powder

Preheat oven to 170 degrees C.
Mix all together into a ball.
Roll out and cut into shapes.
Place on greased baking sheets.
Bake for 12 to 15 minutes.
Leave on tray to cool before moving to a cooling tray.

variation

Divide mixture into two or three; add chocolate to one portion, lemon, vanilla or colouring to another.
Combine the different flavours and colours.
Roll out to give a marble effect.
Cut and bake.

chocolate chip cookies

250g margarine or butter
1 egg
100g sugar
250g flour
1 tsp vanilla
100-150g chocolate chips/drops

Preheat oven to 170 degrees C.
Sieve the flour into a bowl.
Add the margarine, sugar and egg and mix into dough.
Add the chocolate chips to the dough and mix well.
Make large marble size balls.
Place them on a baking tray and press gently to flatten it a little.
Bake for 12 to 15 minutes until golden brown.
Leave on tray to cool before moving to a cooling tray.

storing
You can keep the uncooked dough in a sealed container in the fridge for up to two weeks. Simply take some out, make small balls and place on a lined baking tray and leave on tray for 5 minutes before baking.

cinnamon cookies

1 cup sugar
½ cup butter
1 egg
1 tsp vanilla extract
1½ cups flour
1 tsp baking powder
¼ tsp salt
1½ tsp cinnamon

Mix all the ingredients together.
Make it into a ball.
Cover with cling film and leave in refrigerator for 2 hours.
Preheat oven to 170 degrees C.
Take the dough out.
Make small balls the size of walnuts.
Roll them in cinnamon sugar.
Place on a cooking sheet leaving space for the cookie to spread out while cooking.
Bake for 10 to 12 minutes.

cinnamon sugar

¼ cup caster sugar
1 tbsp cinnamon

eggless chocolate chip cookies

125g butter
125g castor sugar
¼ cup milk + 1 tsp sugar
150g flour
125g chocolate chips

decoration
100g melted chocolate

Preheat oven to 170 degrees C.
Whisk the butter and sugar until light and fluffy.
Stir in the milk mixture, followed by the flour and chocolate chips.
Place spoonfuls on a lightly oiled sheet.
Bake for 12 to 15 minutes or until golden in colour.
Cool slightly before removing from tray.
Decorate with melted chocolate.

ginger biscuits with stem ginger

125g butter
100g caster sugar
75g dark brown sugar
1 egg
250g self raising flour
A pinch salt
1 tsp ginger powder
150g chopped crystallised stem ginger

Preheat oven to 170 degrees C.
Cream the butter, brown sugar and the caster sugar.
Add egg, ginger powder, salt and flour gradually.
Chop ginger pieces and add to the biscuit dough.
Roll into balls.
Dip one side in caster sugar.
Place with sugar side up on a baking sheet.
Press lightly.
Bake for 10 to 15 minutes until golden brown.

melting moments

125g margarine
125g Trex (or cookeen)
1 egg
150g sugar
250g flour
Vanilla
1 tsp baking powder

decoration

Cherries
Oats

Preheat oven to 170 degrees C.
Mix all the ingredients together.
Wet your hands a little. (Wetting hands helps dough from sticking to your fingers.)
Take a little dough and make it into a big marble size ball.
Roll in oats and place on baking sheet.
Press gently to flatten.
Place half a cherry in the centre of the biscuit.
Bake for 12 to15 minute until the biscuits are golden brown.
Leave on tray to cool before moving to a cooling tray.

napolitas

....

150g butter
150g margarine
450g plain flour

Preheat oven to 170 degrees C.
Mix above together.
Roll and cut into shapes.
Bake for 10 to 12 minutes.
Let it cool.
Sandwich two biscuits with jam.

icing
Mix icing sugar with a little water and ice biscuits.

spiced biscuits

250g flour
125g butter
125g brown sugar
1 egg – beaten well
2 tsp mixed spices
¼ tsp grated nutmeg
Pinch of salt

icing

125g icing sugar
1- 2 tbsp hot water
Food colouring

Preheat oven to 170 degrees C.
Beat the butter and sugar together until fluffy.
Add the beaten egg a little at a time.
Sift the flour, salt and spices.
Mix everything together to make dough.
Sprinkle flour on a board and rolling pin.
Roll dough out until ½ cm thickness.
Cut into shapes.
Place biscuits on a greased baking sheet and bake for 12 – 15 minutes or until golden brown.
Cool on wire rack.
Mix the icing sugar and hot water together in a bowl until smooth.
Decorate the biscuits.

sweets

coconut ice
coconut rock – malaysian
coconut toffee – sri lankan
marshmallow
milk toffee
potato toffee

coconut ice

....

1 tin condensed milk
250-300g desiccated coconut
Drops of food colouring

Mix condensed milk and coconut.
Divide into two.
Add colouring to one half of the mixture.
Roll out and place in a square tray.
Roll the other half and place it on top on the first layer.
Leave in the refrigerator to set.
Cut into squares.

coconut rock (Malaysian)

450g grated coconut
2½ cups granulated sugar
¾ cup evaporated milk
¼ tsp salt
4 tbsp butter
½ tsp rose essence
Red food colouring

Line a 22cm tin with grease proof paper.
Put the coconut, sugar, salt and evaporated milk in a large pan.
Stir after 5 minutes.
Cook until it thickens, approximately 15 minutes.
Add the butter and continue to cook for 1-2 minutes.
When the mixture is really thick, add the rose essence and colouring.
The candy is ready when the mixture leaves the sides of the pan, almost like a lump.
To test, roll a small piece into a ball and put it into a glass of water, if the ball does not disintegrate, it is done.
Pour the mixture into the greased tin and flatten top.
Let it cool for ten minutes.
Cut into squares while it is still warm.
Let cool completely.
Lift the grease proof paper with the candy from the tin.
Complete the cutting.

coconut toffee (Sri Lankan)

500g sugar
500g coconut scraped finely
396g can condensed milk
1 cups water
Vanilla
Green food colouring

In a heavy bottomed pan mix the water and sugar.
Keep on low flame and make a thick syrup.
When the syrup is thick, add the coconut.
Keep stirring until it thickens.
Add the condensed milk
Keep stirring on a low flame.
Add flavouring and colour.
Turn off the fire.
Keep stirring until the mixture thickens and leaves the sides of the pan – about 5 minutes.
Spread on a greased tray and mark the pieces while hot.
When cool, cut into pieces.

marshmallows

··

25g gelatine
1 cup water
400g sugar
¼ cup water
A few drops of lemon or lime juice
Corn flour
Icing sugar

Soak the gelatine in one cup of hot water.
Boil the sugar in quarter cup water, add the gelatine.
When it drops from the spoon like a transparent sheet, remove from fire.
Add a few drops of lemon juice and whisk until light, foamy and white.
Add colouring as required.
Pour into a greased tray and set.
When set cut into pieces.
Roll the pieces in a mixture of icing sugar and corn flour.

milk toffee

2 tins condensed milk
250g butter
2 cups of sugar
1 tsp vanilla essence
Chopped nuts (optional)

Mix the sugar and the condensed milk in a pan.
Cook on low flame for about 20 minutes until bubbles start to form on the side of the pan.
Stir continuously.
When the mixture starts to leave the bottom of the pan, cook for another 10 minutes.
Turn off heat and continue stirring for another 2 minutes.
Pour into a greased tray and cut into pieces.

test
Pour a little on a saucer and if the mixture leaves the plate when pushed with a finger –
it is ready.

potato toffee

....

500g potatoes
750g sugar
1-1½ cup of water or milk
2 cardamoms, crushed
50g chopped cashew nuts
4 tsp butter
1 tsp vanilla

Boil potatoes and mash well.
In a pan put sugar and water or milk.
Place the pan on medium heat.
Add the mashed potatoes.
Mix well.
Cook the mixture stir until ready to set. (It takes about 20-25 minutes).
Add cardamoms and cashew nuts, mix well.
Transfer to a greased tray flatten and cut into squares immediately.

glossary

all spice
Also known as Jamaican pepper or pimento.
Its taste is said to resemble a combination of
cinnamon, cloves, nutmeg and pepper. .

anise seed
Also known as anise is a herb with a faint taste
of liquorice and is commonly used Mediterranean
cooking.

aromat
A seasoning of finely balanced blend of herbs and
spices. Can be used like salt and pepper.

banana peppers
Also known as Banana chilli or capsicums is yellow
in colour and has a mild tangy taste.

bay leaves
Gives a bittersweet pungent flavour to dishes. Is
one of the key ingredients for bouquet garni.

bicarbonate of soda
Also known as baking soda

bouquet garni
A bundle of herbs made up of parsley with stalks,
a few sprigs of thyme and a bay leaf.

caijun spice powder
A mixture of spices used in Jamaican cooking.

candlenuts
Must be cooked before eating, as they are
highly toxic when raw. It is often used to thicken
Malaysian and Indonesian dishes. Substitute two
macadamia nuts or Brazil nuts or cashew nuts or
blanched almonds for every candle nut.

capsicum chillies
Another name for green and red peppers.

caraway seeds
Not technically seeds. They are the split halves of the dried fruits of a plant that are used as a spice and have an aromatic distinctive bitter, sharp, nutty taste, with warm, sweet undertones.

cardamom
Cardamom seeds are contained in a pod and have a wonderful aroma with a warm sweet spicy flavour.

cassava chips
Chips made out of tapioca tuber.

chinese cabbage
It has pale, tightly wrapped, succulent leaves with crisp, broad, white ribs and a delicate, mild, sweet flavour.

chinese five spices powder
A mixture of Chinese cinnamon, Sichuan pepper, fennel seeds, star anise and cloves used primarily in Chinese cuisine but also used in other Asian and Arabic dishes.

choy sum
A member of the mustard family. The leaves are juicy and tender and the flavour can be described as midway between cabbage and spinach. It is one of the popular vegetable among the Chinese.

chow chow
Known as chayote squash. The preserved form of chow chow can be purchased at Asian Supermarkets. Substitute melon and ginger jam.

cinnamon
This warm, sweet spice comes from the bark of the cinnamon tree.

cloves
It has a strong sweet but spicy and peppery flavour and should be used in moderation

condensed milk
A cow's milk from which water has been removed. It is most often found in the form of sweetened condensed milk, with added sugar.

corn flour
Also known as corn starch

corn strach
Finely ground part of the corn kernel which is virtually tasteless and used as a thickening agent.

curd
Is made similar to yogurt with buffalo milk.

desiccated coconut
Is coconut meat shredded or flake and dried to remove all moisture. Desiccated coconut can be found sweetened or unsweetened.

edamame
Young soybeans still in the pod. It has a unique flavour. Its taste is between a pea and a lima bean.

galangal
Is a knobbly root from the ginger family. It is mainly used in South-East Asian cooking.

kaffir lime leaf
They are the fragrant leaves of the wild lime tree and are used widely in Thai and South East Asian cuisine. They have a spicy, lemony flavour and give a distinctive citrus scent to soups and curries. Kaffir lime leaves can be substituted with lemon grass.

lemon grass
Also known as sera has a unique flavour and fragrance – lemony but sweet.

longtong
Rice cake cooked in a compressed form.

nutmeg

Nutmeg and mace both come from the nutmeg tree. Nutmeg is the 'nut' and mace is the surrounding skin. It has a warm, spicy aroma and flavour.

pak choy

A member of the cabbage family. The texture of both leaves and stalks is crisp, and the flavour is somewhere between mild cabbage and spinach.

palm sugar

It as originally made from the sap of the Palmyra palm, the date palm or the sugar date palm. Now it is made from the sugar palm and coconut palm.

paneer

A type of soft, crumbly cheese native to India and made with cow's milk.

rampe

Also known as pandan leaf. The juice extracted from the leaves can be used as natural green colouring.

seer fish

It is a firm white fish. It is a type of mackerel found in the regions of India, Sri Lanka. .It's a fairly expensive fish and is considered a delicacy in most places

semolina

Is flour ground from hard durum wheat.

shalots

Small, golden-brown onions. They have a milder flavour than most other varieties of onions.

shrimp paste

Or shrimp sauce, is fermented ground shrimp mixed with salt.

sichuan pepper

It is the dried red-brown berries of a type of ash tree that have a lemony, peppery aroma. It is also one of the spices used in Chinese five-spice powder.

skillet
A skillet's sides flair out and are shallow, whereas a frying pan's sides are straight up. The skillet is deeper and generally comes with a lid.

spring form pan
A type of bake ware that features sides that can be removed from the base.

sago
Comes from the middle part of the trunk of the sago plant. Not to be confused with tapioca.

star anise
A strong anise flavour, with a liquorice-like aroma. It is also used in Chinese five-spice powder.

tamarind
The fruit of the tamarind tree has a sweet sour taste. It is used as a souring agent.

tapioca
Comes from the tuber of the cassava or manioc plant. Also known as Yucca yam.

tofu
It is made from soybeans. It has the ability to absorb flavours through spices and marinades. There are two types of tofu, soft or silken and regular or firm.

vermicelli
Is very fine long strands of pasta which can be made out of wheat or rice flour. In the United States of America is it referred to as Angel Hair pasta.

water chestnut
The edible tuber of a vegetable that grown in the marshes. It has a hint of sweetness.

conversion table

These are approximate conversions. All the recipes are in metric.
Use the imperial measures or metric for a recipe.

oven temperatures

ferenheit	celcius	gas
212	100	¼
250	120	½
275	140	1
300	150	2
325	160/170	3
350	180	4
375	190	5
400	200	6
425	220	7
450	230	8
475	240	9

For Fan Assisted ovens –
Follow manufacturer's guidance

weights

ounces	grams
½	10
1	25
1 ½	40
2	50
2 ½	60
3	75
4	110
4 ½	125
5	150
6	175
7	200
8	225
9	250
10	275
12	350
1lb	450

spoon measurements

imperial	metric
¼ teaspoon	1 ml
½ teaspoon	2.5 ml
1 teaspoon	5 ml
1 tablespoon	25 ml
1 dessert spoon	7.5 ml
¼ cup	50 ml
½ cup	125 ml
1/3 cup	75 ml
¾ cup	175 ml
1 cup	250 ml

volume

fluid ounces	metric
2	55 ml
3	75
5 (1/4 pint)	150
½ pint	275
¾ pint	475
1 pint	570
1 ¾ pint	1 litre

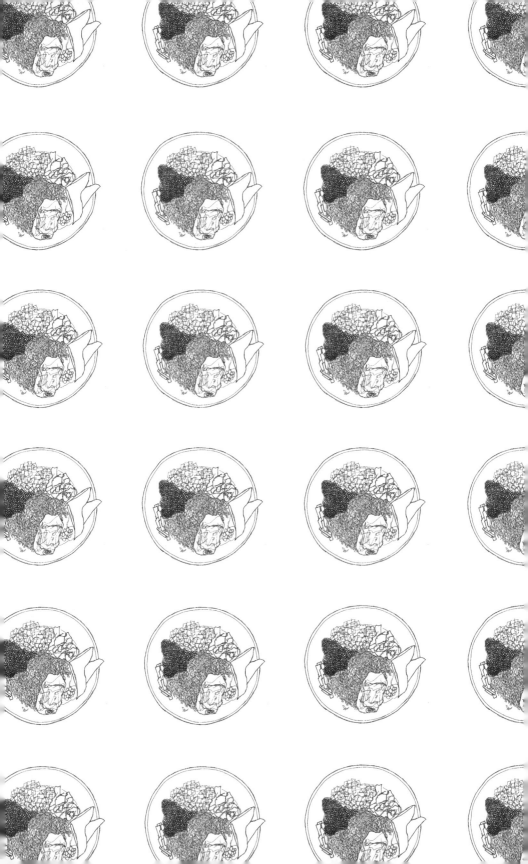

Lightning Source UK Ltd.
Milton Keynes UK
UKOW07f2033091114

241366UK00017B/168/P